CHILDREN'S
ENCYCLOPEDIA
OF BIOLOGY

Tom Jackson

ARCTURUS

Picture Credits:
Every attempt has been made to clear copyright. Should there be any inadvertent omission,
please apply to the publisher for rectification.
Key: b–bottom, t–top, c–center, l–left, r–right

ARCTURUS

This edition published in 2024 by Arcturus Publishing Limited
26/27 Bickels Yard, 151–153 Bermondsey Street,
London SE1 3HA

Copyright © Arcturus Holdings Limited

ISBN: 978-1-3988-3702-7
CH011573US
Supplier 29, Date 0524, Print run 00005916

Printed in China

Author: Tom Jackson
Editors: Becca Clunes, Donna Gregory, and Lydia Halliday
Designer: Lorraine Inglis
Picture research: Lorraine Inglis and Paul Futcher
Consultant: Steve Parker
Design Manager: Rosie Bellwood
Managing Editor: Joe Harris

CONTENTS

Introduction

Biology is the study of living things. Biologists investigate everything about life, but what makes something alive? There are six features of life. Life can move, reproduce, collect nutrients (or food), use an energy source, sense its surroundings, and grow. Some of these features are seen in nonliving things, like cars or crystals, but only something that has all six is truly alive.

Large and Small

There is a lot to discover about living things—from the way tiny microscopic cells work, guided by chemical codes called genes, to how vast communities of plants, animals, and other types of life rely on each other to survive and make Earth a living world.

Classification

To make sense of the huge variety of life, biologists organize all the different species on Earth using a classification system. This system shows how all life on Earth is related, even though evolution has brought millions of species into existence over billions of years.

Human biology

The human body is a collection of systems that each perform a set of vital functions that keeps us alive. For example, the digestive system collects food and turns it into nutrients that the body can use for growth and energy, while the heart, blood, and lungs keep us supplied with oxygen that is used to power life.

Anatomy

This is the study of the way living bodies are structured, and it helps us understand the many different ways a plant or animal can survive. Plants and animals live very different lives and have evolved to inhabit all corners of the globe, from the deep ocean to the dry desert and lush jungles.

Cell Biology

All life is built from tiny units called cells. Each cell is a microscopic living thing filled with busy chemical machines that carry out the processes of life, known as metabolism. A close look at cells helps biologists understand how life as we know it evolved.

Living Together

The biosphere is the region of Earth where life can survive. It is made up of the land and oceans. It also stretches high into the atmosphere and down deep into rocks. The biosphere is filled with finely balanced communities of life called ecosystems. Ecologists study these groups, and they have found that human activities are damaging nature all over the world.

Genetics and Inheritance

Living bodies are complicated. They are constructed according to a set of instructions called genes. The science of genes is genetics. It looks at how the coded instructions are stored on a famous chemical called DNA, and how that code is read and translated into a living body, like your own.

Classification

More than one million species, or types, of living thing have been described by biologists so far, and scientists predict that there are many millions more to be discovered. To make sense of the great variety of life, all organisms are organized into groups using a system called classification.

Connecting With the Ancestors

The aim of taxonomy is to organize all life on Earth according to how the different groups are related to each other. All members of a particular taxon share a common ancestor. That means that all members of a class or order evolved from one species a long time ago. A small group, like a genus, has only a few species, and their common ancestor probably lived quite recently. A bigger group like a phylum has hundreds of thousands of species, and their single common ancestor lived way, way back. The first animal, for example, was a tiny wormlike creature from more than half a billion years ago.

A type of feathered dinosaur is the ancestor of today's birds.

Binomial System

Scientists have given every species a scientific name made of two words. The first word is the generic name, or the name of the genus the species belong to. The second word is the specific name, which is a unique name for that species. This binomial system was created to prevent confusion.

Many of the words used in taxonomy are based on old languages such as Latin and ancient Greek. They often describe the group in some way. For example, bats belong to an order called Chiroptera, which means "hand wings." Our own species name, *Homo sapiens*, means "wise human."

The science of classification is called taxonomy. It divides life into a series of groups called taxons, which are ranked by size. The main basic taxon is the species. A species is a group of living things that can breed and produce young together. For example, all humans belong to one species called *Homo sapiens*.

The human species is part of a larger grouping known as a genus, called *Homo*. There used to be other species in this genus, such as *Homo erectus* and *Homo neanderthalenis*, but they have died out.

The *Homo* genus belongs to a family, Hominidae, that it shares with other great apes: chimpanzees, gorillas, and orangutans.

The hominid family is one of several in the Primate order, which also includes monkeys, lemurs, and gibbons.

Primates are members of the Mammalia class, along with whales, lions, and mice.

TAXON	HUMAN	CHIMPANZEE	BLUE WHALE	SNAKE
Species	*sapiens*	*troglodytes*	*musculus*	*naja*
Genus	*Homo*	*Pan*	*Balaenoptera*	*Naja*
Family	Hominidae	Hominidae	Balaenopteridae	Elapidae
Order	Primates	Primates	Artiodactyla	Squamata
Class	Mammalia	Mammalia	Mammalia	Reptilia
Phylum	Chordata	Chordata	Chordata	Chordata
Kingdom	Animalia	Animalia	Animalia	Animalia

The mammals are one class of the phylum Chordata, which also include reptiles, birds, and fish—anything with a backbone.

All the animal phyla combine to make the Animalia, or animal kingdom. There are several other kingdoms of life on Earth, including plants, fungi, and bacteria.

HALL OF FAME:
Carl Linnaeus
1707-1778

The taxonomy system used today was originally organized by Swedish plant scientist Carl Linnaeus. He set up the system in 1735. It had the same set of taxons as today, but Linnaeus did not understand the process of evolution. Instead he grouped organisms according to how they looked. This led to early mistakes, such as grouping whales and dolphins as kinds of fish, though he later changed this.

DID YOU KNOW? Taxonomists have shown that the fungal kingdom is more closely related to the animal kingdom than it is to the plant kingdom.

Bacteria

Among the smallest and oldest type of life are bacteria. Fossil remains show that bacteria were living on Earth at least 3.5 billion years ago. Bacteria are microscopic organisms and far too small to see without powerful microscopes. They live in all habitats, from the deep ocean to the ice at the top of mountains. They even live in rocks deep underground and float around in the air.

Bacteria evolved at a time when the conditions on Earth were much more extreme than they are now. As a result, bacteria can be found living in places, such as this hot spring, where no other life form can survive. Bacteria also survive in ice and in toxic chemicals.

Single Cells

A single bacterium has a body made of one cell, which is about 2 micrometers long (that's 2 millionths of a meter). The cell is surrounded by a membrane and a rigid cell wall. Inside the cell is held a complex mixture of DNA and other chemicals of life. Most bacteria cells are spherical or rod-shaped but a few have a twisted shape. They sometimes grow into chains or clusters made up of several cells.

One of the most common types of bacteria are the cyanobacteria (also called blue–green algae). Vast numbers of them float in the ocean as plankton. One of the most common species on Earth is *Pelagibacter*. It is estimated that for every human on Earth, there are 3 million trillion of these cyanobacteria in the sea.

HALL OF FAME:
Ruth Ella Moore
1903–1994

In 1933, Ruth Ella Moore became the first Black American woman to earn a PhD in biology. She was an expert in bacteria and worked on the germs that caused tuberculosis—a lung disease that is still one of the biggest killers today. Moore also showed that gum disease and rotting teeth were caused by bacteria in the mouth that lived on sugary foods.

The colors in the water come from the microbes living there and their waste chemicals.

Bacteria, Good and Bad

Some bacteria cause illness such as an upset stomach and sore throat. They can be treated with germ-killing drugs called antibiotics. Bacteria also infect wounds and damage the body, and so they must be cleaned away with antiseptics. However, bacteria are also in foods such as yogurts and pickles. In fact, the bacteria make these foods taste the way they do by adding acids. These food bacteria are useful to the body because they help with digestion. There are billions of bacteria living inside your intestines right now.

Another group of microbes called archaea is found in these hot waters. Archaea look a lot like bacteria and have been around just as long. However, they have a distinct metabolic system, and so form a separate kingdom.

Yogurt is made when bacteria turn the sugars in milk into lactic acid. This gives the sharp taste and creates the gooey mixture.

DID YOU KNOW? The weight of all bacteria on Earth is around 70 billion tonnes (77 billion tons)—45 times heavier than all the world's animals combined!

Protists

The protists are single-celled organisms that have much larger and more complicated cells than bacteria and archaea. Some biologists put all the protists into one kingdom, but they are a varied group of organisms. The cells of protists have many internal structures, just like the cells of multicellular life-forms, such as plants and animals. Some protists live like animals, and others are more plantlike. Some are like both at the same time!

Flagellates and Ciliates

A large group of protists get their name from the flagella and cilia (see page 80) on their cells. Flagellates are a common type of plankton and are responsible for "algal blooms" where seawater is filled with these microbes, choking out other forms of life. Ciliates also live as plankton but are common in soils and even live as parasites inside animals. They waft their cilia to pull tiny particles of food to a mouthlike opening in the cell.

These flagellates have one flagella each, but some have two, three, or several dozen.

Diatoms

These common types of plantlike protists live in seawater and in lakes and rivers. Some species live in damp soil. Diatoms use photosynthesis to make a supply of food from sunlight. They are either rounded or boat-shaped, and the cell sits inside a shelllike case made from silica (the same chemical in sand).

Some animallike protists are called amoebas. The cell has no rigid walls, and so it can squirm into any shape. Many amoebas are parasites that live inside animal bodies, often causing diseases.

The diatom's case is in two halves. The lower half always fits snugly inside the upper one.

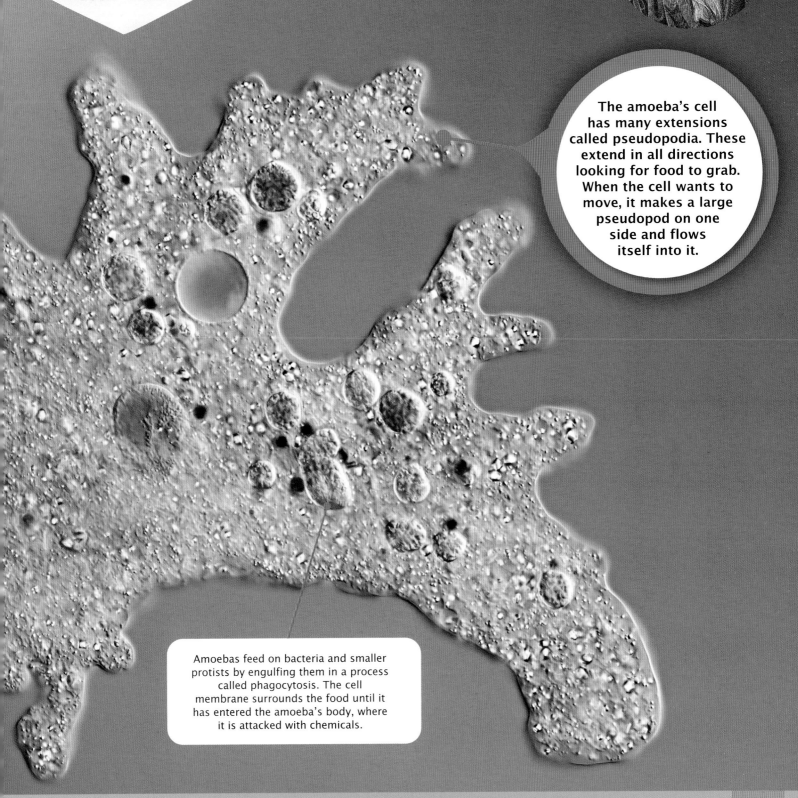

The first person to see protists was Antonie van Leeuwenhoek. This Dutch businessman made much improved versions of the microscope in the 1670s. He discovered a hidden world of microscopic life and called the organisms he saw "animalcules," meaning "little animals." He described many types that we now recognize as ciliates, amoebas, and other kinds of protists.

The amoeba's cell has many extensions called pseudopodia. These extend in all directions looking for food to grab. When the cell wants to move, it makes a large pseudopod on one side and flows itself into it.

Amoebas feed on bacteria and smaller protists by engulfing them in a process called phagocytosis. The cell membrane surrounds the food until it has entered the amoeba's body, where it is attacked with chemicals.

DID YOU KNOW? A protist called *Plasmodium* causes the deadly disease malaria. Each year a quarter of a billion people catch it and around 600,000 die. A new vaccine is being tested to stop *Plasmodium*.

Plants

There are around a quarter of a million species of plants, making up the kingdom Plantae. Members of this kingdom range from tiny mosses to towering trees. Plants power their bodies using a process called photosynthesis. This uses the energy in sunlight to make sugar from water and carbon dioxide. Plants are found in all parts of the world except the coldest and driest habitats.

The giant sequoia is one of the largest and longest-living organisms on Earth. The tree from western North America grows to about 85 m (280 ft) tall and lives for more than 3,000 years!

Internal Vessels

Moss is one of the simplest kinds of plants. It grows over surfaces, and its flat body has no distinct roots, stem, or leaves. Mosses, along with liverworts, are nonvascular plants. Most plants are vascular, which means they have a network of vessels running inside the body. They include ferns, conifers, and flowering plants. The vessels transport water and sugar around the plant. They also make the plant's body stiff enough to grow up toward the light.

The giant sequoia is a conifer. It uses cones to breed and make seeds. Most plants grow flowers, not cones, for this purpose.

Plants like this moss are mostly green because they use a green chemical called chlorophyll to absorb red and blue sunlight and use its energy to make food.

HALL OF FAME:
Janaki Ammal
1897-1984

Born in India, Janaki Ammal studied to be a botanist, or an expert in plants. She was one of the first women to do this. Ammal used her knowledge to breed new kinds of crops that would grow better in India and allow the country to produce its own food. However, she also campaigned to keep as many of India's natural habitats as possible.

Seaweed

The "plants" that live in the oceans are called seaweeds. They are not normally included in the Plantae kingdom. Instead they are algae, types of protists, that grow into large, multicellular bodies. Seaweeds photosynthesize and need sunlight to survive like land plants do, and so they grow mostly in shallow, sunlit water. There are red and brown types, as well as green. Seaweeds have no roots but are anchored to the seabed. Instead of leaves, they have fronds that float in the water.

Seaweeds are exposed to the air when the tide goes out. To stay moist until the sea rises again, many seaweeds cover their fronds in waterproof slime.

Trees use their height to grow above smaller plants so they can collect more sunlight. To grow tall, the trees strengthen their bodies with wood. This is a hardened material made from the internal system of vessels running up inside the trunk.

DID YOU KNOW? Plants make up 80 percent of all the living material on Earth! In total that is 450 billion tonnes (496 billion tons).

Fungi

The Fungi is a third kingdom of multicellular organisms alongside the plants and animals. There are 140,000 known species of fungi. The most familiar are the mushrooms and toadstools that sprout from the ground, but these are only the fruiting bodies that grow to spread the fungus's spores in the water and wind. Most of the fungus is growing unseen below the ground or inside plants—and even on our bodies!

The bright colors of this toadstool are a warning to animals not to eat the fungus. It contains dangerous poisons. Most mushrooms and toadstools will make you sick, so only eat the ones sold in stores.

External Digestion

Fungi are saprophytes, which means they grow on their food. They do not have a mouth or stomach. Instead they release digestive enzymes that break food down into a sloppy mush outside the fungus's body. Then the fungus absorbs the useful nutrients. Fungi are very important members of the natural habitats because they drive the decay of dead material, eating it up and recycling important nutrients into the soil.

This blue-green mold is a kind of fungus. It thrives in damp conditions and grows from microscopic spores that float in the air and land on leftover foods.

Food and Fungus

Many mushrooms are edible and contain minerals and vitamins. Fungi are ingredients in other foods, as well. The blue part of blue cheese is a fungus, and most bread is made with a microscopic fungus called yeast. The yeast eats the sugars in the dough, releasing carbon dioxide gas. Bubbles of this gas make the dough rise and create a soft, springy loaf.

Dried yeast is added to bread dough. Yeast is also used to make beer and wine. The alcohol in these drinks is made by the fungus.

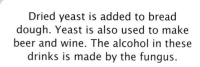

DID YOU KNOW? The largest living thing on Earth is not a mighty whale or a tall tree. It is a honey fungus living in the soil of Oregon. The fungus covers the area of 1,665 soccer fields!

The main body of a fungus is made up of many thin filaments called hyphae. These have stiff walls made from chitin, which is the same chemical used to make insect bodies and crab shells. The network of hyphae is called the mycelium.

Toadstools grow out of the fungus's main body, or mycelium, which is hidden in soil or dead wood. The cap of the toadstool opens up, and microscopic spores are blown away in the wind. New mycelia will grow from the spores.

Toadstools can grow very fast, almost overnight. When the conditions are right, the cells in the stalk will grow longer and longer. This pushes the cap up out of the ground.

HALL OF FAME:
Alexander Fleming
1881-1955

Alexander Fleming, a Scottish microbiologist, made the most important fungus discovery in history. In 1928, mold contaminated his laboratory samples of bacteria. He noticed that the fungus had killed the bacteria around it. The fungus was making an antibiotic chemical, which was later named penicillin. Penicillin and other antibiotics are used today to stop dangerous infections. They have saved hundreds of millions of lives!

Simple Invertebrates

Around 97 percent of animals are invertebrates. An invertebrate is any animal that has no backbone or hard skeleton inside the body (unlike vertebrate animals, such as humans). Instead invertebrates come in a great variety of forms. The simplest of all are the sponges, which form funnel-shaped bodies for filtering food from the water. Other invertebrates include worms, jellyfish, and mollusks.

A sea slug, or nudibranch, is a kind of mollusk that has no shell. Other mollusks without shells include squids and octopuses.

Soft Bodies

The jellyfish belong to a larger group of animals called the cnidarians. They are all soft-bodied animals with tentacles. The tentacles have stinger cells that fire poison darts into anything that touches them. Cnidarians all live in water, and they also include corals and sea anemones. Unlike most other animals, cnidarians do not have a head. Instead their bodies are rounded with a mouth in the middle.

This species is called the fried egg jellyfish. A large jellyfish like this swims by pumping out jets of water by squeezing its bell-shaped body.

HALL OF FAME:
Hope Black
1919-2018

Hope Black was a leading Australian malacologist, or expert on mollusks. She started work at National Museum of Victoria while still a teenager. Within ten years, Black was the first woman to be made a national curator in Australia. In 1959, Black was on one of the first female teams to explore Australia's Antarctic islands.

Mollusks

Mollusks are a large group of invertebrates. Many mollusks, such as snails and slugs, live on land, but most them are aquatic animals. Most mollusks protect their body with a shell. Snails have a single shell, while shellfish like clams and oysters have two shells connected by a hinge.

The mollusk shell is made mostly from a hard stonelike chemical called calcium carbonate. This land snail uses the shell for protection and to keep its body moist.

Like most animals, the sea slug has bilateral body symmetry, which means the right and left halves of its body are mirror images. There is a head at one end where the mouth, brain, and main sense organs are located, and a rear opening for waste at the other end.

The antennae on the head of the sea slug are rhinophores that are used for picking up chemicals in the water.

DID YOU KNOW? A large sea snail called the geography cone shell is one of the most venomous animals in the world. Its venom is 10 times more powerful than a king cobra's.

Arthropods

The largest animal phylum is the invertebrate group called arthropods. That name means "jointed foot," and it refers to how these animals have an armorlike exoskeleton, or hard outer skeleton, made up of interlocking jointed sections. The exoskeleton is made from chitin, a flexible plasticlike material. The arthropods include three main subgroups: the insects, the arachnids, such as spiders and scorpions, and the crustaceans, such as crabs and prawns.

Insects

The insects are by far the largest group of arthropods. In fact, 80 percent of all animal species are insects. Insects have six legs and bodies in three sections: the head, thorax, and abdomen. Often there are one or two pairs of wings on the thorax. It is thought that insects were the first animals to evolve flight around 320 million years ago. Familiar kinds of insects include beetles, flies, ants, and butterflies.

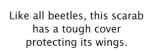
Like all beetles, this scarab has a tough cover protecting its wings.

Wood lice, also called pill bugs, are among the few crustaceans that live on land. However, they only survive in moist habitats such as among fallen leaves. Some species can roll up into a ball to fend off threats.

Crustaceans

Crustaceans have a varied number of legs, and often limblike appendages are used as pincers. Most of these animals live in the ocean. Copepods and krill, two types of crustaceans that live as plankton, are among the most numerous animals on Earth. Larger crustaceans like lobsters toughen their exoskeleton with calcium carbonate. Other crustaceans include barnacles that glue themselves to a rock and filter food from the water with their feathery legs.

DID YOU KNOW? Very few kinds of insects live in the sea. The main group is called the sea skaters. All others live on land or in fresh water.

The arachnids have eight legs and limblike mouthparts called palps. All arachnids are hunters, and most kill using venom. The venom turns the prey to mush which the arachnid then slurps up through their small mouth.

Like all arachnids, this spider has two body sections. The legs are attached to the forward section, called the cephalothorax. The rear section is the abdomen. Unlike other arthropods, arachnids have no antennae or feelers on the head.

Spiders use silk to catch prey. This one has created a netlike web of sticky silk that snares flying insects. The spider uses its feet to pick up any vibrations made by prey or other spiders.

HALL OF FAME:
Margaret S. Collins
1922–1996

Margaret S. Collins was such a clever child that she was allowed to start attending university at the age of 14. She became only the third Black American woman to become a doctor of zoology. Collins became an expert in termites—wood-eating insects that live in huge colonies. Termites can damage houses made from wood, and Collins wanted to learn as much about them as she could. Collins was also a leading figure in the Civil Rights Movement in Florida.

Lower Vertebrates

Amphibians spend the first stage of their life in water swimming around as fishlike tadpoles. They then grow legs and transform into adults that move out onto the land.

The first vertebrates were fish that evolved around 500 million years ago. All of today's vertebrates (animals with backbones and internal skeletons) evolved from fish. The first land vertebrates were amphibians—the ancestors of today's frogs and salamanders. These land animals evolved into reptiles and the ancestors of mammals. Birds evolved later from dinosaurs (a type of reptile).

Reptiles

The reptiles are a varied group. They all have skin covered in tough waterproof scales, and they are not reliant on water to breed (unlike fish and amphibians). There are three major types: the turtles and tortoises, the crocodiles, and the squamates. This last group is by far the largest and contains snakes and lizards. Most reptiles lay eggs with a waterproof shell, but a few give birth to their young. They are ectotherms, or cold-blooded, meaning their bodies are the same temperature as the surroundings.

Snakes have evolved to slither on their bellies without legs. There are about 4,000 species, and 600 of them, including this blue viper, use venom to kill prey.

HALL OF FAME:
Bertha Lutz
1894–1976

Born in Brazil and educated in Paris, France, Bertha Lutz became a leading expert in poison dart frogs. These brightly colored little amphibians collect poisons from the ants and other insects that they eat and store them in their waxy skin. The poisoned skin makes any predators sick—or even die—so they learn not to attack the frogs. Alongside her career as a zoologist, Lutz helped ensure Brazilian women were allowed to vote and was also involved in setting up the United Nations. Two frog species and four lizards are named after her.

The gills are located behind the head. Water enters the mouth, flows through the gills (where oxygen is transferred to the blood), and then out through slits on the side of the neck.

Fish

There are 33,000 species of fish. They live in the oceans and in freshwater rivers and lakes. They use gills to take oxygen from the water, although a few species can breathe air for short periods. Fish have a basic streamlined body that flows easily through the water. There is a tail fin for swimming and a number of side fins for steering. The back, or dorsal, fin stops the fish from rolling onto its side as it swims.

All frogs are hunters. The horned frogs of South America have mouths that are large enough to swallow prey that is the same size as the frog!

Adult frogs have no tails. They move by hopping, while salamanders and newts keep their tails into adulthood. Amphibians return to water to breed. Their eggs have no shells and will dry out unless they are laid on or under the water.

DID YOU KNOW? The marine iguana is the only lizard to feed under the sea—it eats seaweed. When food is scarce, the lizard shrinks in size to save energy.

Birds

There are around 10,000 species of birds, most of which are capable of flight. All of them have two legs and a pair of wings. To take to the air, a bird's body must balance low weight with great strength. Flightless birds, such as ostriches and penguins, do not have this issue. The ostrich has swapped flight for a large size and great running ability, while penguins use their wings as flippers for swimming, not flying.

Birds have no teeth. Instead the mouth is formed by a hard beak or bill. The shape of the beak indicates what food the bird eats. Hooked beaks are for ripping and cracking foods. A pointed beak is best suited for picking up small items, like insects.

Primitive Birds

The birds evolved from dinosaurs around 150 million years ago. The descendants of these first birds are known as fowl and include waterbirds, like ducks and geese, and ground birds, like chickens and this partridge (right). Waterfowl are strong fliers that often make long migrations by air. The mute swan is one of the largest flying birds of all. However, ground birds spend most of their time feeding on the ground and are only capable of short fluttering flights to escape danger.

The shape of a bird's wing shows how they fly. The square wing of this eagle is ideal for soaring and slow, controlled flight. Smaller triangular wings are for faster flight with tighter turns.

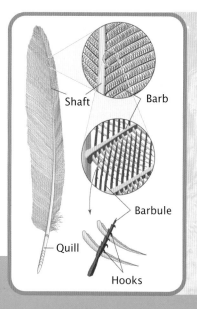

Shaft   Barb

Barbule

Quill

Hooks

Feathers

The first animals to have feathers were dinosaurs. These animals used them for warmth. Birds do this, too. The feathers near the skin are small and fluffy and trap a blanket of warm air. Feathers are made from keratin, the same material in mammal hair and reptile scales. Wing and tail feathers are flat and stiff because the many branches of keratin are neatly linked together.

Bird skeletons have no tail section. However, the birds create a tail with long feathers. The tail helps with flying. It is used for steering and braking. Some birds use their long tails to communicate and get attention.

Songbirds, like this multicolored tanager from South America, often have brightly colored feathers. This is to make it easier for mates to find each other. Many birds also sing regularly to advertise their presence.

HALL OF FAME:
John James Audubon
1785–1851

This French–American artist and naturalist is famous for making an extensive record of all North American birds and painting each species. John James Audubon published his full set of pictures from 1827-38, and they are still a good way of identifying birds. The National Audubon Society was set up in his name to protect birds in North America and across the world.

DID YOU KNOW? The hooded pitohui from New Guinea is one of the world's only poisonous birds. It collects poisonous chemicals from its ant food and stores them in the skin.

Mammals

The most varied and widespread vertebrates are mammals. All mammals have hairy bodies for at least some of their lives, and they all feed their young on milk. Beyond that, they come in all shapes and sizes. The smallest mammals are the size of a thumb, while the largest—the 24-m (79-ft) blue whale—is as long as two buses. Mammals are warm-blooded, which means they use energy from food to maintain a constant body temperature. As a result, mammals can survive everywhere from the icy polar seas and high mountains to steamy jungles and dry deserts.

This antelope calf is an example of a hoofed mammal. These plant-eating mammals have long legs tipped with tough hooves, which are the equivalent of very thick toenails. Thanks to their long legs, most hoofed animals are fast runners.

Marine Mammals

Some mammals have returned to live in the oceans. They have lost their legs and can no longer walk on land. Instead their limbs are flippers, which are much more useful in the water. Marine mammals include the cetaceans, such as dolphins and whales, which have lost their back legs entirely and never come on land. There are also the pinnipeds, better known as the seals and sea lions, which return to beaches to rest and are able to shuffle short distances on land.

Like all cetaceans, dolphins have smooth skin (they have hairs before they are born) and a nostrillike blowhole on top of the head for breathing at the surface.

Hair is made from shafts of dead cells coated in keratin. It grows from a root embedded in the skin. Keratin is also used to make fingernails, claws, and hooves. Some animals have a coating of keratin to make the skin waterproof.

DID YOU KNOW? The musk ox is the mammal with the longest hairs. Some of the hairs grow to 1 m (40 in) long. The musk ox lives in the Arctic. Its long hair forms a thick curtain against the cold wind.

Marsupials

Most mammals are born after developing for some time inside their mother's uterus (womb). Female kangaroos and other marsupial mothers have a small uterus. Their babies are born early in their development, when very small. The baby, or joey, then moves to a pouch on the mother's belly, where it drinks milk and continues its development. Marsupials are the main kind of mammal in Australia, although there are marsupials living in North America and South America, too.

Kangaroos do not walk. Instead they hop along on their large, bouncy back feet. This is an efficient way to get around, especially when carrying a big joey in the pouch.

The cheetah is the fastest running animal of all. It can reach speeds of 110 km/h (68 mph), but only for a few seconds. All that exertion makes the cat very hot, and it has to stop and cool down.

HALL OF FAME:
Jane Goodall
1934–

When she was 26 years old, Jane Goodhall went to live alongside a group of chimpanzees in the forests of Tanzania. She watched how the apes behaved and communicated, and she built up a picture of how chimp society worked. One discovery Goodhall made was that chimpanzees constructed simple tools to collect food. Ever since, Goodhall has been studying primates and calling for wild places to be better protected.

Homeostasis

All living bodies use a system called homeostasis, which means "stay the same." The human body is constantly working to keep internal conditions just right for its processes to function as well as possible. The system is mainly focused on keeping its temperature, water content, and chemical balance more or less constant.

Keeping Warm

A normal human body temperature is around 37°C (98°F), which is generally warmer than the surrounding air. That means the body is always losing heat, and must find ways of slowing that process and staying warm. When the body temperature falls too low, the main muscles will start to twitch. This process is called shivering. These moving muscles give out warmth, which helps to keep the body temperature from falling dangerously low.

Wearing thick clothes on a cold day helps by trapping a layer of air against the body. Heat moves slowly through this layer of air, so the body stays warm.

Goose Bumps

The human body is covered in hairs—just as many as our close relatives like chimps and gorillas have. However, the body hairs are generally much shorter and harder to see. In cold conditions, each hair stands upright making "goose bump" lumps on the skin. The upright hairs trap a layer of still air against the skin, reducing heat loss.

A goose bump is created by a tiny muscle just below the surface of the skin. The muscle pulls on the hair shaft to make it erect, and that pushes up a bump on the surface.

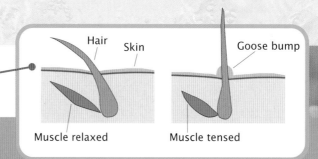

Hair   Skin   Goose bump

Muscle relaxed   Muscle tensed

The phenomenon of homeostasis was fully investigated by this American doctor around 100 years ago. Walter Bradford Cannon also described the fight or flight response. This is when the body switches from being relaxed to being ready to respond to danger. A hormone called adrenaline is released, which changes the internal body conditions in a matter of seconds, redirecting energy to the muscles and senses.

Osmoregulation is the area of homeostasis involved in keeping the right amount of water in the body. We become thirsty when we need more water. Excess water is removed in urine.

On warm days, the body must get rid of the heat created by life processes. Sweating is the main cooling system. Water spreads over the skin and takes away the heat as it evaporates.

The blood vessels in the skin are involved in thermoregulation, or the control of body temperature. On cold days, they shrink in width so less blood flows through them, and the skin goes pale. On warmer days, the vessels expand letting more blood through. The skin becomes redder as this blood gives out its heat.

DID YOU KNOW? While it is possible for the human body to go without eating for three weeks before becoming seriously ill, it cannot survive for longer than three days without a supply of water.

Digestion and Excretion

The body needs a frequent supply of chemicals for fuel and to use as raw ingredients for growing and maintaining the body. These materials come from our food, and digestion is the process that breaks down the food into useful substances. Waste materials are then removed using a process called excretion.

Digestive Tract

Digestion's job is to turn the complex substances in food into simpler chemicals that can be absorbed by the body. This process has many steps that take place in the digestive tract, which is a long tube that passes through the body from the mouth to anus. Chemicals called enzymes break up the food, and it is absorbed into the blood in the small intestine.

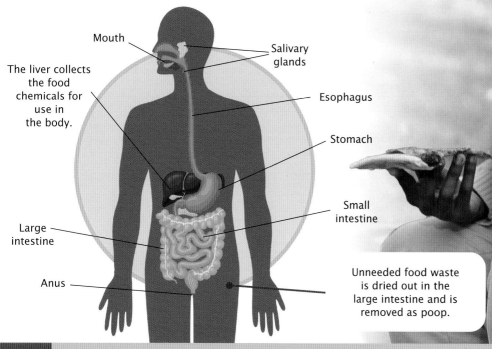

Mouth

Salivary glands

The liver collects the food chemicals for use in the body.

Esophagus

Stomach

Small intestine

Large intestine

Anus

Unneeded food waste is dried out in the large intestine and is removed as poop.

After swallowing, food is mashed up in the stomach. It is in there for about four hours as it is mixed with powerful chemicals that turn solid foods into a thick mushy liquid.

DID YOU KNOW? The small intestine is only 3.5 cm (1.5 inches) wide and about 7 m (23 ft) long, but its inner lining is covered in tiny hairlike extensions. If these extensions were made flat, they would cover a tennis court.

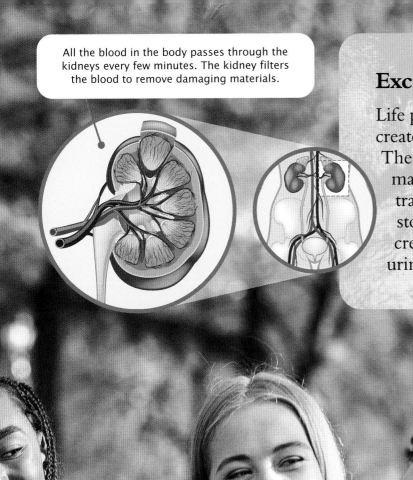

All the blood in the body passes through the kidneys every few minutes. The kidney filters the blood to remove damaging materials.

Excretion

Life processes taking place inside the body create waste products that have to be removed. The kidneys collect unwanted chemicals to make a water mixture called urine. Urine travels along tubes to the bladder, where it is stored. When the bladder is about half full, it creates the urge to urinate (or pee), and the urine is emptied out.

Digestion starts as the teeth chew up food into smaller chunks. Saliva is added in the mouth to make smooth balls of food that are easy to swallow.

HALL OF FAME:
Santorio
1561–1636

The link between food and digestion was proven by a long experiment carried out by this Italian scientist over 30 years. Santorio built a weighing chair so he could keep a record of his weight before and after every meal and every time he used the toilet. He also weighed his meals, his urine, and his poop. Santorio's data showed that the weight of the food did not equal the weight of the waste. Some of the material from the food was going into his body.

Food and Diet

Like all animals, humans survive by eating food. Food is made from the bodies of other living things, mostly plants, animals, and fungi. Whatever the source, food is composed of the same kinds of chemicals that are all useful to the body.

These foods contain starch, which is a kind of complex carbohydrate. Simple carbohydrates are sweet sugars, and the sugars combine into larger forms to make starchy foods like bread and pasta.

Food Groups

There are three main types of food. Carbohydrates include sugars and starches. They are used as the main source of energy for the body. Fats and oils belong to a food group called lipids. These are used by the body as an energy store. The brain is also 60 percent fat. Proteins are complex chemicals used inside every cell and in muscles. The proteins in foods can be broken up into smaller building blocks, which can be rebuilt into whatever type of protein the body needs.

PROTEIN
The meat of animals is a good source of protein and fats, although these food groups can be found in plants and mushrooms as well.

HALL OF FAME:
James Lind
1716-1794

This Scottish naval doctor carried out a famous experiment that showed the importance of vitamins. British sailors were dying from a disease called scurvy after eating poor diets on long voyages. James Lind tried to discover which fresh fruits made them healthy and found that limes helped. It was later discovered that limes and other citrus fruits contain a lot of vitamin C, which prevents scurvy.

FRUIT AND VEGETABLES
Plant foods also contain a food group called fiber. This is actually a special complex carbohydrate called cellulose, which humans cannot digest. Instead the fiber passes right through, helping to keep the gut strong and healthy.

Vitamins

The body is able to manufacture most of the chemicals it needs from the main food groups. However, it also needs a small but frequent supply of 13 vitamins. These are essential chemicals that are needed for the body to work properly but some of which cannot be made by the body. It is important to eat a wide range of fresh foods to get all the vitamins you need.

A baby's first food is milk. Some people keep drinking milk from cows, sheep, and goats for their whole lives, and they eat other dairy products made from this milk, such as cheese and yogurt.

Many meals make use of grains, such as rice, corn, and wheat. They can be made into breads, noodles, and pasta or eaten as they are.

SUGARS
Simple sugars taste sweet. The sugar can coat the teeth, where bacteria produce acids that damage the tooth's hard coating. Always brush your teeth 30 minutes after eating sugars.

DID YOU KNOW? At least 1,900 species of insects are safe for humans to eat. Around two billion people worldwide regularly eat insects, such as locusts and crickets.

Respiratory System

The body needs a constant supply of oxygen from the air. It is the job of the respiratory system to provide it. The respiratory system includes the airways and the lungs. Air coming into the lungs exchanges some of its oxygen with carbon dioxide, a waste gas that is breathed out.

Air entering the lungs is 21 percent oxygen. The air that comes out is only 16 percent oxygen.

Breathing Cycle

On average, you inhale (breathe in) and exhale (breathe out) every four seconds. The process is controlled automatically, mostly by a large muscle called the diaphragm. To breathe in, the diaphragm flattens. It stretches the lungs downward. Air flows in from the nose and mouth to fill the extra space. To breath out, the diaphragm bends upward and squeezes the air out.

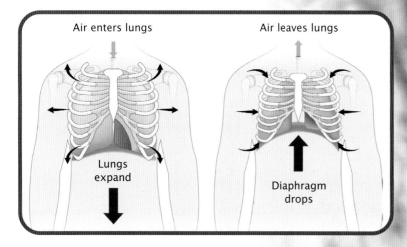

Air enters lungs

Air leaves lungs

Lungs expand

Diaphragm drops

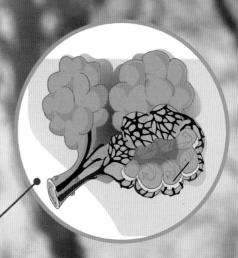

Each lung is full of sacs called alveoli that are surrounded by blood vessels. Oxygen in the air moves to the blood. Carbon dioxide in the blood moves the other way.

DID YOU KNOW? The world record for someone holding their breath belongs to Budimir Šobat from Croatia. In 2021, he breathed in pure oxygen and held his breath underwater for 24 minutes!

Coughs and Sneezes

When there is a blockage or an irritation of the airways, it is cleared with a cough or sneeze. These work by drawing in a big inbreathe and then closing off the airways using a flap in the throat called the epiglottis. (Normally the epiglottis's job is to keep food from going into the lungs.) With the epiglottis closed, the air pressure inside the lungs builds up. Once released, the surge of air will push the blockage out of the way.

The breath also includes water vapor from the moist lining of the lungs. This vapor forms cloudy breath on cold days.

During a sneeze, the tongue is used to block the mouth so that all the air is forced out of the nose.

On average, a human breathes 13,500 liters (2,970 gallons) of air every day. That's enough to fill 85 barrels.

HALL OF FAME:
Galen
129–216

This Greek doctor had the job of treating wounded gladiators after deadly fights in the Colosseum in Rome. Galen got to see a lot of the internal structures of the human body. He also cut up dead animals, like pigs, to learn more. Galen used bellows to pump air into the lungs, and he was the first doctor to show how they were connected to the throat by a windpipe, or trachea. He also identified that the larynx, or voice box, is at top of the trachea.

Circulatory System

The blood supply is the human body's transportation system delivering oxygen and food to all body parts and taking away the waste. The heart pumps blood around the body along tubes or vessels. Together these body parts make up the circulatory system.

It is important to exercise regularly so that the heart and circulatory system stay healthy. Any exercise that makes you feel tired out will help.

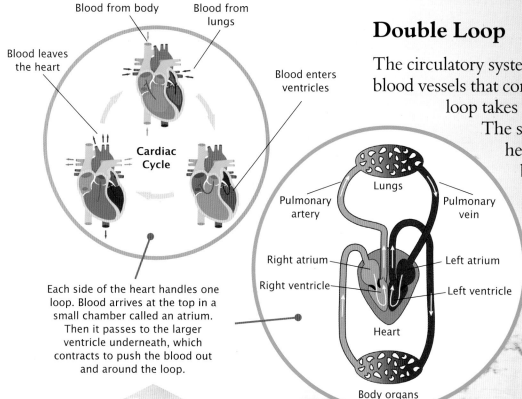

Blood from body

Blood from lungs

Blood leaves the heart

Blood enters ventricles

Cardiac Cycle

Each side of the heart handles one loop. Blood arrives at the top in a small chamber called an atrium. Then it passes to the larger ventricle underneath, which contracts to push the blood out and around the loop.

Lungs

Pulmonary artery

Pulmonary vein

Right atrium

Left atrium

Right ventricle

Left ventricle

Heart

Body organs

Double Loop

The circulatory system is made of two loops of blood vessels that connect to the heart. The larger loop takes the blood around the body. The smaller loop connects the heart to the lungs, where the blood can collect fresh oxygen and discharge carbon dioxide.

HALL OF FAME:
William Harvey
1578–1657

Ancient doctors believed that the blood spread out from the heart and was absorbed by the body, and new blood is being made all the time. William Harvey, a doctor who looked after the British royal family, thought this did not make sense. He was not allowed to examine dead human bodies, so instead he experimented with animals. In 1628, he confirmed what others had already suspected—that blood circulates around the body in closed loops.

Blood Vessels

Blood is carried away from the heart by vessels called arteries. They are lined with muscles that pulsate in time with the heart beat to push blood along. This can be felt as a pulse. Blood returns to the heart along veins. These have valves that ensure that blood only moves in one direction.

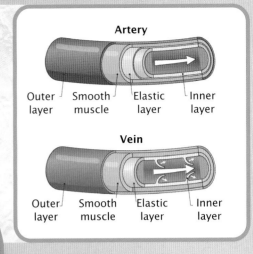

Artery

Outer layer · Smooth muscle · Elastic layer · Inner layer

Vein

Outer layer · Smooth muscle · Elastic layer · Inner layer

Most of the blood is made up of disk-shaped red blood cells. These carry oxygen using a red chemical called hemoglobin.

A normal resting heartbeat for an adult is between 60 and 100 beats a minute. Children's hearts beat faster than adults.

The heart rate and breathing rate increase as the body moves faster and does more work. This ensures that the body takes in oxygen more rapidly to power the activity.

DID YOU KNOW? The average volume of human blood is 5 liters (10 pints). It takes just 45 seconds for the heart to pump all of this blood around the body.

Skeleton

The human skeleton contains 206 bones. At birth, we have 270 bones, but as we grow older, several smaller bones fuse together to make larger ones. The skeleton is the internal framework of the body. It is there to give the body its shape, to create a protective cage around the soft organs, and to create solid anchor points for muscles and ligaments.

Joints

The place where two bones meet is called a joint. The human skeleton has 340 joints, although most of those are fixed and inflexible. All body movements happen as flexible or synovial joints. The bones are connected by elastic straps called ligaments. There are six kinds of synovial joints in the human body, each one able to move in different ways with twists, bends, and swivels.

The main body has the axial skeleton. This is made up of 80 bones including the flexible spinal column of 33 vertebrae, 24 ribs, and the skull, which is a brain case made of 21 bones fused together.

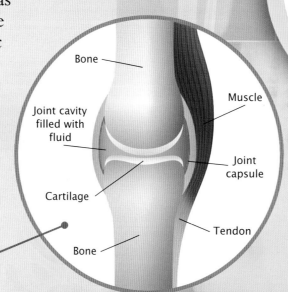

Bone

Muscle

Joint cavity filled with fluid

Joint capsule

Cartilage

Bone

Tendon

The place where the bones meet is surrounded by a fluid-filled capsule. The tips of the bones are also padded with soft cartilage tissue.

HALL OF FAME:
Mary Leakey
1913–1996

The Leakey family is famous for discovering fossil skeletons belonging to the distant ancestors of modern humans that lived in East Africa millions of years ago. Mary Leakey discovered the skeleton of an early relative of African apes, including chimpanzees, gorillas, and humans, that lived in the area about 20 million years ago.

DID YOU KNOW? The smallest bone in the body is not connected to the skeleton. It is the 2-mm (0.08-in)-long stapes, or stirrup bone, that is used to transmit sound through the ear.

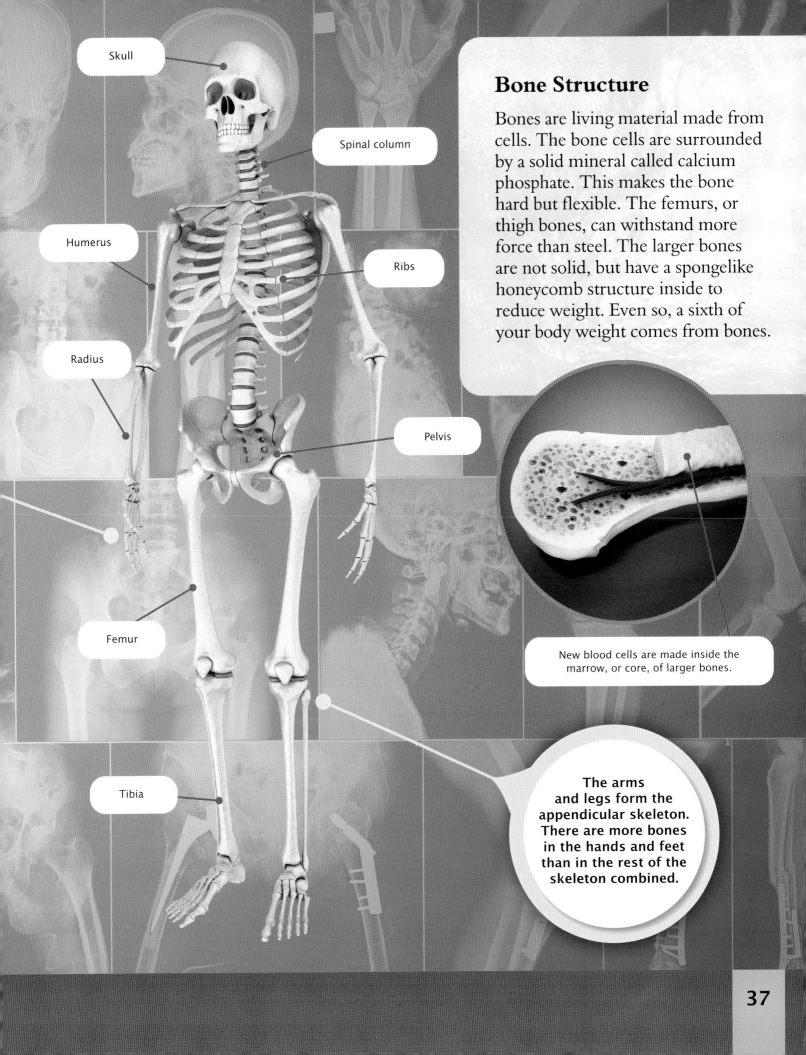

Skull

Spinal column

Humerus

Radius

Ribs

Pelvis

Femur

Tibia

Bone Structure

Bones are living material made from cells. The bone cells are surrounded by a solid mineral called calcium phosphate. This makes the bone hard but flexible. The femurs, or thigh bones, can withstand more force than steel. The larger bones are not solid, but have a spongelike honeycomb structure inside to reduce weight. Even so, a sixth of your body weight comes from bones.

New blood cells are made inside the marrow, or core, of larger bones.

The arms and legs form the appendicular skeleton. There are more bones in the hands and feet than in the rest of the skeleton combined.

Muscles

There are hundreds of muscles in the human body, consisting of three types. Cardiac muscle is only found in the heart, and it doesn't get tired like other muscles, so it can keep working all the time. Smooth muscle is used in the gut, arteries, and other tubes. Skeletal muscles, of which there are around 650, are used to move the body.

Muscles cannot contract forever. The muscle cells create lactic acid as they work hard to contract, and this acid makes the muscle burn and feel tired. Eventually it must relax.

Moving Joints

Muscles create forces by contracting, or growing shorter, so they cannot push, only pull. As a result, skeletal muscles work in pairs to move joints, with one of the pair contracting while the other stays relaxed. One muscle, the flexor, contracts to bend the joint. On the other side of the joint, the extensor muscle contracts to straighten the joint.

Muscles are made up of billions of microscopic protein fibers bundled together.

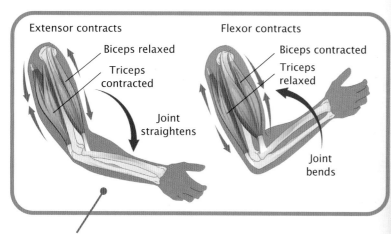

Extensor contracts

Biceps relaxed

Triceps contracted

Joint straightens

Flexor contracts

Biceps contracted

Triceps relaxed

Joint bends

The muscle is attached to bones by connectors called tendons. The tendon does not stretch much at all, so all of the force from the muscle is transferred to moving the joint.

HALL OF FAME:
Luigi Galvani
1737–1798

In 1780, Italian scientist Luigi Galvani found that the muscles of frogs contracted as an electric current flowed through them. Galvani thought that electricity was made by the living force of an animal—and it was still there, for a while at least, after it had died. The discovery led to the invention of the battery, and also much later it was shown how contractions were stimulated by the movements of electrical charges in muscle cells.

Food

Esophagus

Sphincter

Stomach

Smooth Muscle

The muscles that push food through the gut are called smooth muscle. It is less strong than skeletal muscles. Smooth muscle is either longitudinal, meaning its fibers all line up, or it is circular, so fibers are in rings. These two types work together to create rhythmic waves of contractions in the gut that push food along.

The waves of contractions in the gut are called peristalsis. For this to work best, the food in the gut needs to contain solid fiber, so the muscles have something to push against.

Exercising muscles makes them bigger and stronger. By working a muscle hard, the fibers become a little damaged. The muscle gets stiff as they mend, and they grow back bigger than before.

When a joint bends too much, the ligaments that connect the bones together become stretched. This injury is called a sprain. The best thing to do is rest the joint so the ligament can recover.

DID YOU KNOW? The smallest muscle in the body is the stapedius muscle—it is only 1 mm (0.04 in) long. It pulls on the tiny bones inside the ear, helping to reduce the effects of loud sounds.

Nervous System

The nervous system is the main way that different parts of the body communicate. It is in two parts. The central nervous system is made up of the brain and the spinal cord. The peripheral nervous system is a network of wirelike nerve cells that spreads through the body. These nerve cells collect information from the senses and send it to the central nervous system. The brain sends back a response through the nerves to the muscles and other body parts if necessary.

Lobes of the Brain

The outer layer of the brain is called the cerebral cortex. It is very large in humans and is divided into four lobes, or regions. Thoughts and decision-making are handled by the frontal lobe. Vision is processed by the occipital lobe, while the parietal and temporal lobes are linked to speech, memory, and the other senses.

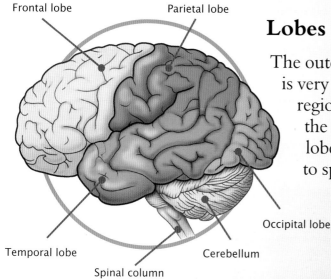

Frontal lobe

Parietal lobe

Occipital lobe

Temporal lobe

Cerebellum

Spinal column

The cerebellum low down at the back of the brain is a filter system that ensures muscle movements are smooth and coordinated.

Sensory nerves bring signals to the central nervous system, while motor nerves carry them away.

Reflex Action

Not all movements are controlled by the brain. Sometimes muscles work by a reflex, which is controlled by the spinal cord. The recoil reflex pulls the hand away from a sharp or hot object. A nerve signal does not go all the way to the brain but instead loops through the spinal cord to the arm muscle, creating a "reflex arc." The reflex ensures that action is taken as soon as possible to prevent injury.

Pain receptor

Pain signal goes to brain

Brain

Sensory nerve

Relay nerve

Motor nerve

Spinal cord

Muscle moves hand away

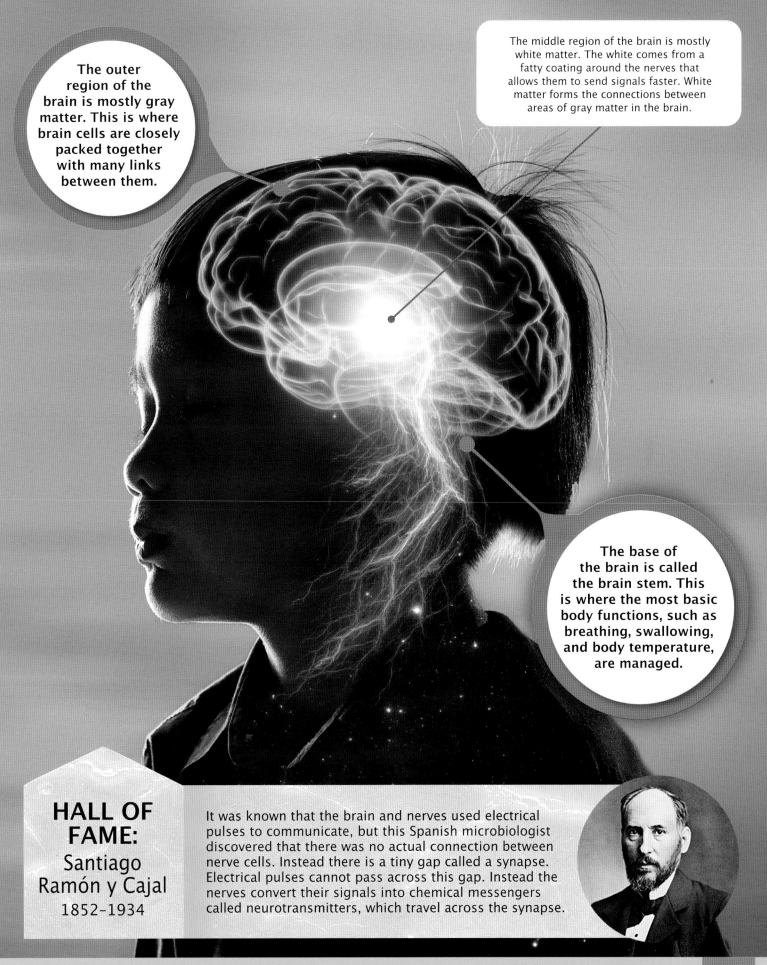

The outer region of the brain is mostly gray matter. This is where brain cells are closely packed together with many links between them.

The middle region of the brain is mostly white matter. The white comes from a fatty coating around the nerves that allows them to send signals faster. White matter forms the connections between areas of gray matter in the brain.

The base of the brain is called the brain stem. This is where the most basic body functions, such as breathing, swallowing, and body temperature, are managed.

HALL OF FAME: Santiago Ramón y Cajal 1852–1934

It was known that the brain and nerves used electrical pulses to communicate, but this Spanish microbiologist discovered that there was no actual connection between nerve cells. Instead there is a tiny gap called a synapse. Electrical pulses cannot pass across this gap. Instead the nerves convert their signals into chemical messengers called neurotransmitters, which travel across the synapse.

DID YOU KNOW? If the human brain was a computer, it would have a storage capacity of 2.5 petabytes, or 2.5 million gigabytes.

The Senses

The human body is said to have five senses: touch, sight, hearing, taste, and smell. However, this is simplifying the situation a lot. The human senses are constantly collecting information about what is going on inside and around the body. All this information is processed by the brain to create our sense of awareness.

There are millions of touch receptors in the skin that pick up different kinds of forces pushing on the skin, such as sharp pricks or hard pressure.

Sense of Vision

The eye works a lot like a camera to capture images. Light beams pass through the pupil at the front and are focused onto the light-sensitive retina at the back of the eye by the cornea and flexible lens. When light hits a cell in the retina, it stimulates a nerve signal. Many of these signals together create a record of the image formed by the eye, and this record is sent along the optic nerve to the brain for processing.

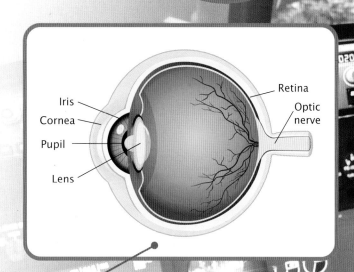

The iris can open and close to control the amount of light entering the eye. It opens wide in dark conditions and tightens up in bright light.

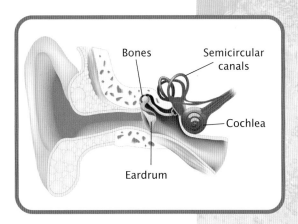

Sense of Hearing

Sound is the result of vibrations in the air. The ear is a highly sensitive touch organ that can pick up these waves, or movements in the air, and convert them into nerve signals. The wave enters the outer ear and makes the eardrum vibrate. That vibration is passed to three tiny bones, which tap out the vibration onto the cochlea. This is a spiral of fluid, and the sound wave ripples through it, wafting hairlike nerve cells that send out signals to the brain.

DID YOU KNOW? The human nose seldom detects one chemical at a time. Instead each odor is a mixture of many chemicals. The nose can distinguish around 1 trillion distinct odors.

Nasal cavity

Smell receptors

Nostril

Mouth

Tongue

Windpipe

The senses of smell and taste use chemical detectors on the tongue, gums, and inside the nasal cavity. The tongue can pick up at least five tastes, and the nose can pick up 10,000 distinct chemicals in the air.

The ear is also involved in the sense of balance. The brain detects changes in head position by the way fluid shifts the semicircular canals in the inner ear. When this fluid gets churned up, we feel dizzy.

HALL OF FAME:
Ibn al-Haytham
965–1040

Also known as Alhazen, this medieval scientist from what is now Iraq conducted the first scientific experiments to show that the eyes detect beams of light arriving from the surroundings. Before Ibn al-Haytham's work, most people believed that the eyes sent out invisible flashes that scanned objects and reflected back. Al-Haytham's work with mirrors and lenses also helped to show how light was focused inside the eye into a sharp image of the scene in front of it.

Immune System and Diseases

The body is under constant attack from other organisms that are trying to get inside. Organisms that damage the body and cause diseases are called pathogens. They include bacteria, viruses, fungi, and even worms. The job of keeping pathogens out, and hunting down any that get in, belongs to the immune system.

The immune system needs to work fast to fight pathogens. It raises the body's temperature so the metabolism runs faster. A fever, or high temperature, is a clear sign that someone is sick.

Clotting

The skin is the first line of defense against attack. The outer layer is constantly shedding from the body and taking germs and dirt with it. Germs can get in through a cut in the skin, and this is sealed up quickly by clotting, where the blood forms a solid patch called a scab.

The scab is a network of solid protein strands. It gradually dries out and flakes off as the skin underneath is repaired.

White Blood Cell

If pathogens get into the body, it is the job of white blood cells to find and destroy them. There are several kinds of white blood cells. Some produce chemical markers called antibodies that stick to the attackers. Other blood cells then destroy anything with these marks. Memory cells keep a record of pathogens, so they can be dealt with if they infect the body again.

DID YOU KNOW? An allergy, such as hay fever or asthma, is caused by the immune system mistaking a harmless substances, like pollen, for a pathogen and responding to an attack.

The immune system uses a lot of the body's energy, which is why being sick makes us feel tired.

Pathogens can spread to all parts of the body. The lymph system is a set of tubes running through the body that drains liquids from the muscles and organs, and filters out pathogens.

HALL OF FAME:
Ozlem Tureci
1967–

This German doctor is one of the scientists that created vaccines for Covid-19, a new disease that killed 7 million people between 2020 and 2023. Ozlem Tureci's vaccine was able to teach a person's immune system how to fight back against Covid, so they would be less sick and less likely to die from the disease.

Reproductive System

A human baby develops inside its mother's uterus, or womb, before being born. The baby starts life in a process called sexual intercourse. The penis, a male sex organ, enters the vagina, one of the female reproductive organs, and leaves behind sperm. This sperm moves to the uterus and combines with an egg cell produced by the mother. Together they make the first cell of a new human.

Doctors who look after mother and child during pregnancy are called obstetricians. Midwives are also medical carers who are experts in helping women give birth.

Male Sex Organs

Sperm are produced inside the testes, small egg-shaped organs housed inside the scrotum, a sac hanging beneath the penis. The sperm are transported along tubes to the prostate gland, where they are combined with liquid called semen. During intercourse, the penis is filled with blood, which makes it longer and harder so it fits into the vagina, where the semen and sperm are released.

Prostate | Seminal vesicle | Bladder
Vas deferens
Uretha
Penis
Testicle | Epidydimis

The penis also contains the urethra, a tube that connects to the bladder. Urine leaves the body through the urethra.

Fallopian tubes
Uterus
Fimbriae
Ovary
Endometrium
Cervix
Vagina

Female Sex Organs

Eggs, or ova, are made by rounded organs called the ovaries. Every month, an egg is released from one ovary, and it travels to the uterus via the fallopian tube. The uterus has been made ready for a baby to develop inside if this new egg meets a sperm. If not, the uterus will shed its lining. This process is called menstruation, or a period. It restarts the process of preparing for the next egg to arrive.

The opening of the uterus is called the cervix. During intercourse, the cervix allows sperm inside. It becomes tightly closed once a fetus starts to develop inside.

In 1864, Rebecca Lee Crumpler became the first Black American woman to become a doctor. She became a specialist in child development and the care of women and babies after birth. She was working at a time after the American Civil War when enslaved people were being made free. Many white American doctors would not treat people who had been enslaved, and Crumpler worked for the government helping to provide them with care.

Ultrasound scanners send high-pitched sounds into the uterus. The sounds, which are harmless and too high to hear, echo off the fetus so the parents and medial experts can see it is healthy.

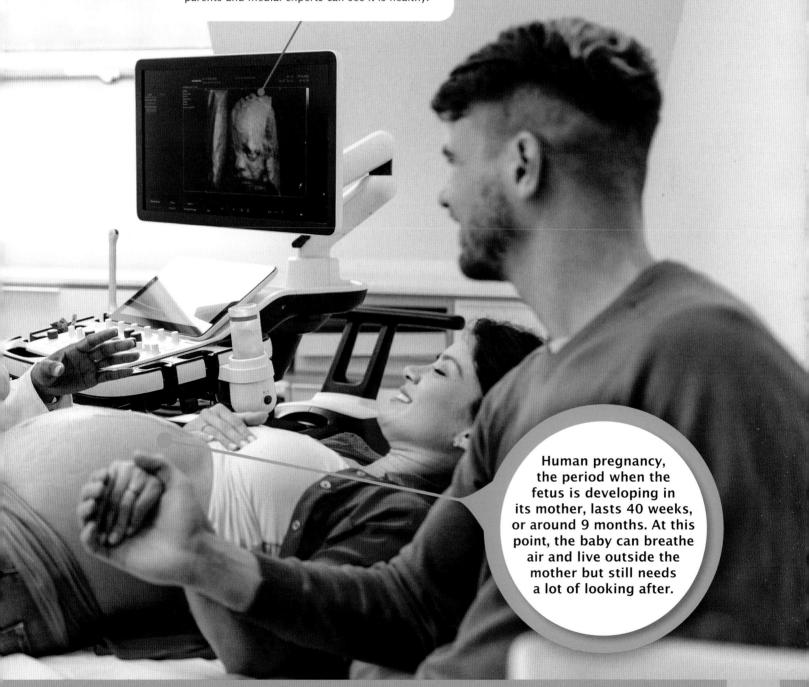

Human pregnancy, the period when the fetus is developing in its mother, lasts 40 weeks, or around 9 months. At this point, the baby can breathe air and live outside the mother but still needs a lot of looking after.

DID YOU KNOW? In 2021, Halime Cissé from Mali became the only mother of nonuplets in history when she gave birth to five girls and four boys.

Growth and Development

Girls reach their full adult size around the age of 15, while boys stop growing taller at 18. Even so, the brain and nervous system will continue to develop until around the age of 24. The fastest period of growth is while a baby is still in the uterus. A single microscopic cell develops into a 3-kg (6.6-lb) baby in 280 days.

The fetus does not breathe or eat in the uterus. Instead it is provided with what it needs by the placenta. Inside the placenta, oxygen and nutrients move from the mother's blood to the baby's.

Three Trimesters

A baby developing inside the uterus is called a fetus. Its development happens in three-month stages, or trimesters. In the first trimester, the fetus develops all its body parts and organs. The fetus's body is mostly fully functioning by the end of the second trimester. If it is born around this time, the baby could live, as long as it got good medical care. The third trimester is devoted to growth and adding fat under the skin.

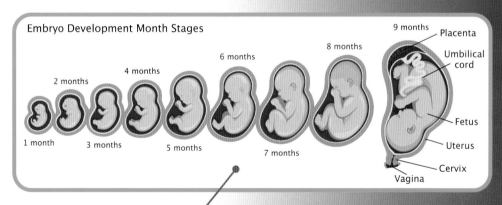

Embryo Development Month Stages

1 month · 2 months · 3 months · 4 months · 5 months · 6 months · 7 months · 8 months · 9 months

Placenta · Umbilical cord · Fetus · Uterus · Cervix · Vagina

In the ninth month, the fetus rolls over so that its head is pushing down on its mother's cervix. This weight helps to signal that the baby is ready to be born.

HALL OF FAME:
Cleopatra the Physician
1st century CE

Not a lot is known about this female doctor and writer from ancient Greece. She wrote one of the first books on gynecology, which is the medical study of the female reproductive organs. Cleopatra also wrote extensively on other ailments suffered by women and suggested using medicines such as roasted horse teeth, mouse droppings, and deer bone to cure them.

Childhood

In the first year after birth, a child will double in height and triple in weight! They are half their adult height by the age of two but do not reach half their adult weight until they are about ten.

Childhood is the first 10 years for girls and 12 years for boys. After that, children enter puberty, where their growth speeds up again, and they develop adult body features.

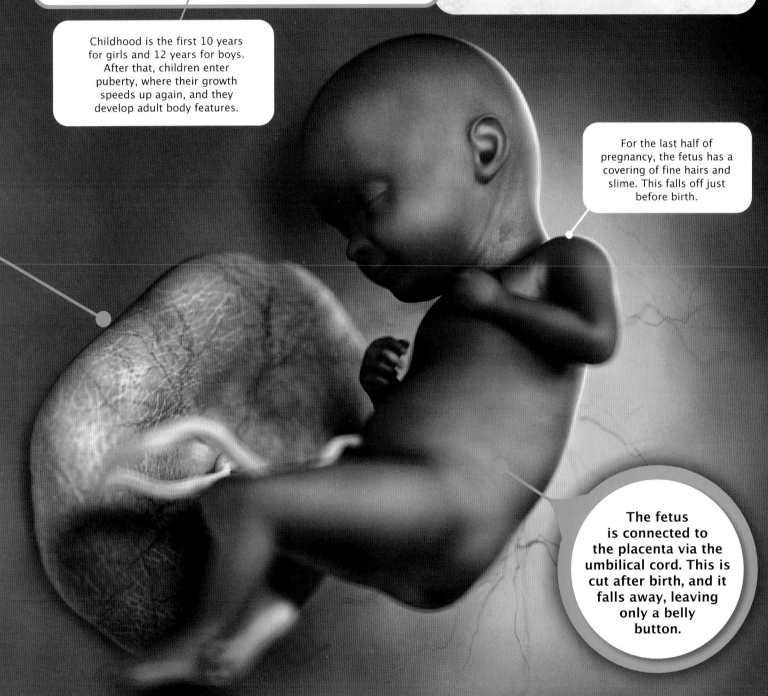

For the last half of pregnancy, the fetus has a covering of fine hairs and slime. This falls off just before birth.

The fetus is connected to the placenta via the umbilical cord. This is cut after birth, and it falls away, leaving only a belly button.

DID YOU KNOW? Only 5 percent of babies are born on time. The rest arrive early or late.

Photosynthesis and Respiration

All life on Earth requires a source of energy to power its metabolism, or life processes. The energy used by life is delivered by two processes, photosynthesis and respiration. Photosynthesis is used by plants to convert the energy in sunlight into sugar fuels. Respiration releases the energy in sugars for use in metabolism.

Chloroplasts

Membrane stack

Photosynthesis occurs in plant cells inside green capsules called chloroplasts. They are green because they contain the pigment chlorophyll. When sunlight hits the chlorophyll, some of its energy is absorbed. This energy is used to react carbon dioxide gas from the air with water to make a simple sugar called glucose. The reaction produces oxygen as a waste product, and this is given out by the plant. The same process of photosynthesis occurs in some bacteria, but bacteria do not use chloroplasts to hold chlorophyll.

Chlorophyll is bonded to stacks of membranes inside the chloroplast. This molecule looks green because it absorbs red and blue light but reflects back the green beams.

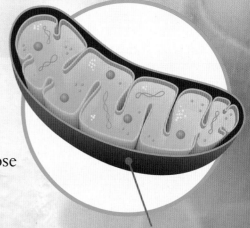

Mitochondria

Respiration is more or less the reverse of photosynthesis where oxygen reacts with glucose to release energy as it breaks up into carbon dioxide and water. In complex life, respiration happens inside structures in the cell called mitochondria. The glucose and oxygen react in several small steps so energy is released slowly. The carbon dioxide produced by respiration must be removed from animal bodies, although plants can use it again for photosynthesis.

Mitochondria are surrounded by two membranes. Respiration happens close to the inner one, which is highly folded to increase its area.

Plants are autotrophs, or "self eaters," because they use photosynthesis to create their own food supply. They use this food in respiration whenever needed.

Animals are heterotrophs, or "other eaters." They survive by eating the body parts of other organisms, using respiration to release energy from this food.

This hummingbird is using a lot of energy to hover as it feeds. Muscle cells have many thousands of mitochondria to release the energy they need.

HALL OF FAME:
Jan Ingenhousz
1730-1799

Photosynthesis was discovered by this Dutch biologist in 1779. At this time, scientists were only just beginning to understand that air was filled with separate gases, such as oxygen and carbon dioxide. They also knew that plants gave out these gases in different conditions. Jan Ingenhousz showed that oxygen is made when a plant is in sunlight, but that this stops when it gets dark.

DID YOU KNOW? Before photosynthesis evolved around 3.5 billion years ago, there was no oxygen in the air. In fact, oxygen was poisonous to most living things back then.

Plant Bodies

Plants range in size from the mightiest tree to the tiniest daisy, but they follow the same basic body plan. The lower part is made of roots that extend into the soil. The middle of the plant is a stem that often divides into branches before sprouting leaves on the upper part of the plant.

The older xylem tubes in thicker stems are filled in with a hard material to make wood. Woody stems, or trunks, are very strong, and so plants can grow to heights of more than 100 m (330 ft).

Transport Vessels

Most plants have an internal network of vessels that run up the stem between the roots and leaves. Xylem tissue carries water and dissolved nutrients and salts. It is made from dead cells with open ends, and so forms stiff tubes that also provide structural support to the plant. Phloem tissue transports sugars, the plant's energy source, from the leaves where they are made to the rest of the plant.

Water always flows upward along xylem, while the sugars in phloem can travel in either direction.

Leaf Anatomy

A leaf is a plant's solar panel and is thin and flat, so that it catches as much light as possible. The light enters through the top, and here the cells are packed with chloroplasts to capture its energy. The water needed for photosynthesis is provided by vessels in the leaf's central vein. Carbon dioxide from the air enters gas spaces in the lower part of the leaf through pores called stomata.

The stomata are mostly on the underside of the leaf to prevent water from evaporating away rapidly in strong sunlight.

DID YOU KNOW? Pando is a forest of about 40,000 aspen trees in the United States that are all connected underground, making it the world's largest plant.

HALL OF FAME:
Agnes Arber
1879–1960

Agnes Arber became interested in botany, or the science of plants, while still at school. After a long education, she became a full-time scientist and started to publish books on plants. These works were groundbreaking in the way they described plant bodies scientifically. Arber was an expert in conifers and grasses.

Roots need a supply of air as well as water. These mangrove trees have sturdy woody roots above the water, so they can access the air.

Bark is not quite the same as wood. It has waxy chemicals in it to make it waterproof, and there are often smelly oils and resins that ward off insects and other invaders.

Plant Reproduction

The two main types of plants that grow on land—the flowering plants and conifers—reproduce by making seeds. Seeds are created when pollen grains carrying male sex cells fuse with female ovules (which hold the egg cells). During this process, known as pollination, pollen is moved from plant to plant by the wind, water, or animals.

Flowers use bright colors and powerful odors to attract insects and other animals. The animals come to eat nectar, a sweet liquid produced the by the flower.

Stigma
Ovary
Stamen
Petals

Flowers

The flower is a plant's sexual organ. Pollen is produced on tall stalks called stamens, while the ovules are held in the ovary in the center of the flower. Wind-pollinated flowers produce dry, dustlike pollen that blows away easily. Flowers that rely on animals, such as insects, for pollination create sticky grains that cling to animal bodies. Pollen from another flower sticks to the central stigma and burrows into the ovary.

After pollination, the ovary develops seeds, and the surrounding region grows into a fruit of some kind. The fruit is designed to spread the seeds somewhere they can grow.

HALL OF FAME:
Karl von Frisch
1886-1982

Honeybees are famous for dancing. The dance is a way for one honeybee to communicate to others the direction and distance to a good foraging location full of flowers. Karl von Frisch, an Austrian biologist, discovered the honeybee dance and translated what it means. He won the Nobel Prize in 1973 for this important breakthrough.

DID YOU KNOW? The smallest pollen is made by the forget-me-not flower. It is about 6 microns (0.006 mm), about the same size as a bacterium.

Germination

The process by which a seed sprouts into a new plant is called germination. Germination is stimulated by temperature, water levels, and the length of daylight. When conditions are right, a shoot will emerge from the seed and grow toward the light and away from gravity. The seed contains one or two embryonic leaves called cotyledons, which contain a store of nutrients that fuels growth until the first true leaves can form and start to photosynthesize.

Leaves

Cotyledon

Stem

Seed

Root

The plant's first root, the radicle, does the opposite of the stem. It grows toward the pull of gravity and away from light.

Honeybees are one of the most important pollinators. The bees carry nectar and pollen back to the nest. The nectar and pollen are the raw ingredients for making honey, the bees' main food.

Animals carry pollen grains from flower to flower, where they can be used in reproduction. Some of the animals will eat the pollen as well, but there is plenty to spare.

Plants in Extreme Habitats

Plants can grow wherever there is light, water, and nutrients in the soil. There are many habitats across the world where these things are in short supply, and plants have had to evolve special body parts and lifestyles to survive in these extreme habitats.

Dry Conditions

Plants that live in deserts spend most of the year waiting for rain. When rain does fall, the water trickles rapidly through the loose soil of sands and stones, so the roots of desert plants spread out sideways, making a net that collects water from a wide area. After the rain, the desert plants are in a race to flower and produce seeds before the land dries out again. The seeds will lie in the dry soil and germinate during the next wet season.

Living stones from the deserts of southern Africa are plants with just two fleshy leaves that look like pebbles.

Cold and Dark

Cold places are just as dry as a desert because all the liquid water is frozen into solid ice. The winters in cold parts of the world are also long and dark, and the plants that live there, such as conifer trees like pines, only grow during the short summer when the ice melts. There is no time for conifers to grow fresh leaves in spring, so the trees are evergreen, meaning that they keep their leaves all year round.

Conifer leaves are shaped like needles. This keeps the leaves from being damaged by frosts in winter.

HALL OF FAME:
Sylvia Edlund
1945–2014

Sylvia Edlund was a Canadian botanist who spent many years studying the plants of the Arctic. The habitat there is tundra, where most of the soil is permanently frozen all year round. Only the top layer melts in summer, allowing small plants to sprout for a few weeks. Edlund discovered areas of lush plants in hidden valleys among the tundra that were fed by the water from melting snow.

Cacti are common plants in American deserts. They have thick stems and branches that have a fleshy interior that acts as a store of water. The whole plant is green because every part is able to photosynthesize.

A large cactus has a deep root that will reach down to damp soils far underground.

The cactus does not have obvious leaves. Instead they grow as sharp spines. Instead of working to make food, the spines protect the plant from animal predators.

DID YOU KNOW? *Welwitschia* are plants that grow in southern Africa. They only have two leaves, but these are 4 m (13 ft) long. *Welwitschia* live for more than 2,000 years.

Animal Bodies

There are thought to be several million animal species, although most are still unknown to science. Each one has evolved to live in a unique way in a specific habitat, and so there is huge diversity in their shape and size. One thing animals have in common is a body that is capable of actively moving to gather food.

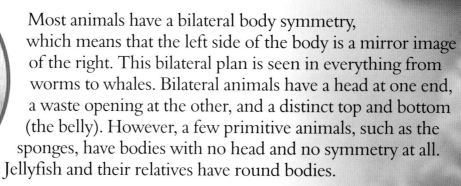

Fish have a solid internal framework, or skeleton, made from bone and cartilage. This gives the animal its shape.

Body Symmetry

Most animals have a bilateral body symmetry, which means that the left side of the body is a mirror image of the right. This bilateral plan is seen in everything from worms to whales. Bilateral animals have a head at one end, a waste opening at the other, and a distinct top and bottom (the belly). However, a few primitive animals, such as the sponges, have bodies with no head and no symmetry at all. Jellyfish and their relatives have round bodies.

This centipede's body is constructed from several repeating segments. Many animals have a body organized like this, with different segments specializing for different tasks.

Frequent Changes

Animal bodies can change a lot through the life cycle of species. All kinds of animals, from insects to frogs, have a larval phase, where the young animals look very different to the adults and survive in a completely different way. For example, a caterpillar larva eats leaves while an adult butterfly sips nectar. Similarly, mammals and birds will develop thicker coats of hair or feathers in winter and shed them for a cooler covering in summer.

This snow monkey keeps warm on cold winter days by taking a bath in warm, volcanic springs. Its fur has also become much thicker but will thin out in spring.

HALL OF FAME:
Pierre Belon
1517–1564

This French zoologist was one of the first scientists to study comparative anatomy. Pierre Belon compared the body structures of different animals, such as humans and birds, to look for what made them different and which body parts were the same. This process was an important step in understanding how animals—and all other kinds of life—are always evolving.

Sea anemones are named after a type of plant (anemones are pretty flowers). Early biologists thought they were seaweeds, but sea anemones are all meat-eating killers!

The sea anemone has no hard body parts. Instead it has a hydrostatic skeleton made up of capsules of water. These capsules are flexible but retain their shape. This gives the anemone's muscles something to pull against.

DID YOU KNOW? The longest animal in the world is not the blue whale (that's the largest) but the siphonophore. These close cousins of jellyfish have tentacles 45 m (150 ft) long, almost twice the length of a whale!

Animal Locomotion

There are several forms of animal locomotion—the most primitive is swimming. This generally involves the movement of the whole body to push the animal through the water. Some animals, such as squid, propel themselves with jets of water. Walking, running, and climbing all make use of legs and feet, but many land animals get around without them.

Moving by jumping is called saltation. Kangaroos are famous for moving like this. The animal leans forward and raises its long tail to stay balanced in the air.

Air Time

Animal movement over land often involves spending time off the ground in the air. During walking, at least one foot is on the ground at any time. Running is faster, so all the animal's feet are off the ground for short leaps. Gliding is a not quite the same as flying. It is a slow, controlled fall from a high start point to a lower landing site. Expert gliders, such as sugar gliders, can stay in the air for several seconds.

True flight is when the wings create a life force that allows animals to travel up away from the ground. Only four types of animals have evolved true flight: insects, bats, birds, and pterosaurs. (This last group became extinct along with the dinosaurs.)

HALL OF FAME:
Eadweard Muybridge
1830–1904

Eadweard Muybridge was a pioneer of moving images. He used many cameras set out in a line to take photographs in order. Together, they could be made into an early form of video. Muybridge used his system to capture the way animals, mostly horses, moved. His videos showed how the legs moved differently when the animal walked, trotted, and galloped.

Slithering

The snake is a familiar example of a legless animal, but others include caterpillars, worms, and maggots. There are three main ways a legless animal can slide. In rectilinear motion, the body ripples in an up-down wave as it slides forward. In the second method, the body loops from side to side as it pushes on the ground. The third method is sidewinding, where the wavelike body movements push the animal sideways instead of forward.

Sidewinding is useful for moving efficiently over loose ground like desert sand.

The forelimbs are free for holding food, cleaning fur, and boxing rivals!

Kangaroos are known as macropods, meaning "big feet." The tendons connecting the feet to the leg muscles are very stretchy, so the animal bounces without having to use much energy.

DID YOU KNOW? Young spiders create sails of electrified silk strands to catch the wind and take to the air. They can travel long distances using this method, which is known as ballooning.

Animal Reproduction

The aim of life is not just to survive but to reproduce and increase in number. Animals will divert their resources to reproduction, often going without food in order to succeed. Sexual reproduction is the most common method for animals, where each new individual has two parents, but there are nevertheless many different strategies to get the best results.

This aphid is giving birth to daughters using asexual reproduction. The baby insects have no father, only a mother, so she can produce offspring very quickly without needing to find a mate.

Aiming for Quantity

Smaller animals often devote their resources to producing large numbers of young. The females produce large numbers of small eggs, and the males generally fertilize them after they are released. The parents have little ability to take care of large numbers of young, and inevitably many will die before they are able to breed themselves. However, this strategy allows just a few animals to rapidly populate a new habitat if that opportunity were to appear.

Frog spawn is left unguarded in the water. The eggs will hatch into tadpoles that must fend for themselves, and most will not make it to adulthood.

HALL OF FAME:
Aristotle
384–322 BCE

The way animals reproduce was not fully understood until the early twentieth century, when the science of genetics and inheritance showed how DNA was passed from parents to offspring. Long before that, people believed that small animals, like worms and aphids, emerge spontaneously from rotting material. This idea was first put forward by Aristotle, a Greek philosopher, who some say was one of the first biologists. He made detailed records of sea life in the waters near his home.

DID YOU KNOW? The oceanic sunfish produces 300 million eggs each year. Only a tiny fraction—perhaps one or two—of these eggs will reach full adult size.

Orangutans have the longest childhood of any wild animal. The mother spends nine years raising each of her children.

Parental Care

An opposite reproductive strategy is to have only a few young at one time and invest time and resources into protecting them. This maximizes the chances of them reaching maturity and having a family of their own. Humans use this strategy. The babies of animals that use this system are often born very helpless and require the mother and father to carry them and find their food. Eventually, the offspring will learn to do this for itself.

All the baby aphids are genetically identical clones of their mother. They are already growing daughters of their own inside them as they are born.

Asexual reproduction means that aphids (also called greenfly) can spread fast, covering a plant in just a few days.

Other Senses

Some animals have different senses that appear to give them superpowers compared to how humans view the world. Snakes can see prey from the glow of their body heat, sharks can find hidden prey from the electric pulses they give out, while bats can find their way in the dark using sounds.

Heat Sensors

Several types of snakes, most notably pit vipers, have patches of heat-sensitive skin on their snouts. Heat rays, also called infrared radiation, give a kind of invisible light that our eyes cannot detect. Our skin can feel heat—to avoid fires or stay out of the hot Sun—but the vipers' pits are able to detect the body heat of prey in the dark.

Pit viper venom is slow-acting, so prey often runs off after a bite. The viper can keep track of its meal using heat sensors and follow the victim until it dies.

The shark, like many aquatic animals, has lateral line sensors. These run down the side of the body and are highly sensitive to the motion of the water flowing past them. Lateral lines detect the water currents made by other fish swimming nearby.

Echolocation

Bats hunt mostly at night. Many catch small flying insects in midair. To see these prey would require very large eyes, which are too heavy for these little flying mammals. Instead bats give out high-pitched calls that echo off the insects and surroundings. The bats pick up the echoes with their large ears and use them to figure out what is around them in the dark.

A bat's call is so loud that the ears close up to prevent being deafened. They open again to listen for echoes.

This Italian scientist was one of the first to use a microscope to investigate how animals worked. He discovered many important features about the kidneys, lungs, and blood vessels. Marcello Malpighi was also the first person to see the electroreceptors on a shark's snout. However, these sensors are named the "ampullae of Lorenzini" after another Italian who gave a more detailed description.

The flat snout of the hammerhead shark is covered in gel-filled holes that pick up the faint electrical fields created by the bodies of other animals. The wide hammerhead allows the shark to scan the water and pinpoint where the animals are, even buried in the sand.

The mantis shrimp is able to detect not just three colors—red, green and blue—like a human, but 12! This includes ultraviolet light, which is invisible to us.

The shark's skin has tiny toothlike spikes that allow it to slice through the water.

DID YOU KNOW? Two-thirds of a shark's brain is devoted to processing smell information. It can pick up blood in the water from 400 m (437 yd) away.

Studying Cells

One of the basic laws of biology is called cell theory. It says that every living thing has a body made of at least one cell—often many billions—and every one of those cells developed from an older cell. To understand how bodies work, we need to look more closely at cells.

The scientists that study cells and other tiny forms of life are called microbiologists. To see even more detail, they use electron microscopes.

Microscopes

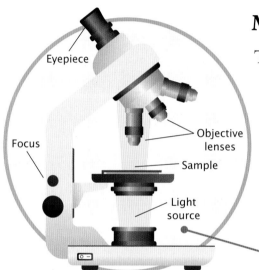

Eyepiece

Focus

Objective lenses

Sample

Light source

The main tool for studying cells is the light microscope. It works by using two sets of lenses to magnify tiny objects so they can be seen in detail. Light shines up through the sample and is focused inside the microscope by the first lens into a tiny but highly detailed image. The lens in the eyepiece then magnifies that image so it is big enough for the human eye to see.

A biological microscope generally has three objective lenses, each giving a different level of magnification.

Preparing a Sample

The best way to examine cells is to place a very thin slice of tissue on a clear glass slide. This slice is bathed in a droplet of water, and a see-through cover is placed on top. This holds the sample still and flat so that the lenses can focus. Dyes are added to the water to highlight features of the sample. Salts and other chemicals can also be used to investigate how the cell operates.

The sample is thin enough for light to shine right through. So the view through the microscope is a silhouette of the cells.

HALL OF FAME:
Margaret Pittman
1901–1995

Margaret Pittman's start in science came as a child when she assisted her father, who was a doctor, with his patients. She excelled at school and college and worked as a teacher to save money to go to the University of Chicago, where she became an expert in bacteria and microbiology. She worked well into her 70s, investigating the bacteria involved in deadly diseases like cholera and meningitis.

The scientists can adjust the brightness and position of the light source to get a different view of the cell samples.

A pipette is used to add dyes or other chemicals to the sample.

DID YOU KNOW? A light microscope can see objects that are 200 times smaller than the width of a human hair.

Plant Cell

Plants and plantlike protists have a distinctive cell structure that sets them apart from other kingdoms of life. The most obvious feature is the cell wall that surrounds the cell's outer membrane and provides structural support. Additionally, the cells in the green parts of a plant have chloroplasts that are used for photosynthesis.

Internal Structures

All cells share some basic features. The contents of cells are in a watery liquid called cytoplasm, which is all contained inside an enveloping cell membrane. The cells of complex life, such as plants, have a nucleus where the DNA is stored. As well as chloroplasts and a cell wall, plant cells typically have a large vacuole. This is a bag used to store water, salts, and sugars.

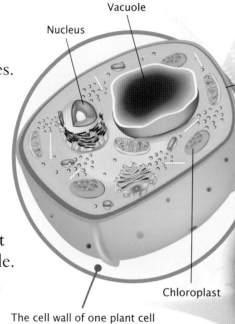

Vacuole

Nucleus

Cell membrane

Cell wall

Chloroplast

The cell wall of one plant cell is glued to its neighbors to create strong plant bodies.

The wooden board is composed of dead plant cells made of cellulose walls filled with another hard polymer called lignin.

Hay, or dried grass stalks, is almost pure cellulose. Farm animals have stomach bacteria that can digest this tough material.

Tough Cell Wall

The plant cell wall is made from a carbohydrate called cellulose. This is a polymer, or chainlike chemical, that is made from smaller glucose molecules linked together. The structure of cellulose makes it a very sturdy substance that makes plant bodies strong enough to stand upright. Cellulose is left behind after all the other parts of the cells have rotted away.

DID YOU KNOW? Plant cells are roughly rectangular. They are generally between 0.01 and 0.1 mm (0.0004–0.004 inches) long.

HALL OF FAME:
Robert Hooke
1635–1703

This English scientist was one of the first people to use a microscope. In 1665, he used it to study a thin piece of cork (from the bark of a cork oak tree) and saw that it was made from many tiny compartments. Robert Hooke thought that these compartments looked like the cramped living quarters of monks, known as cells, and that term has been used every since.

An onion is a plant body part called a bulb. Bulbs allow a plant to store food underground in winter so it can sprout again in spring.

The individual cells of a thin layer of onion skin are easy to see under a microscope. These have been dyed so the starch food stores in the cells show up as purple.

Animal Cell

An animal cell has no cell wall, just a flexible outer cell membrane. As a result, the cells have no standard shape and take many forms. Like the cells of a plant and fungus, animal cells have several types of internal structures called organelles.

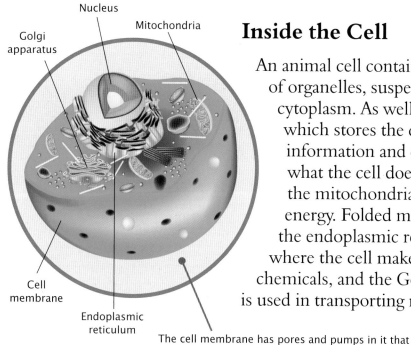

Golgi apparatus

Nucleus

Mitochondria

Cell membrane

Endoplasmic reticulum

The cell membrane has pores and pumps in it that allow materials to enter and leave the cell.

Inside the Cell

An animal cell contains several kinds of organelles, suspended within cytoplasm. As well as the nucleus, which stores the cell's genetic information and determines what the cell does, there are also the mitochondria for producing energy. Folded membranes called the endoplasmic reticulum are where the cell makes its useful chemicals, and the Golgi apparatus is used in transporting materials.

The skin is also called the epidermis. Epidermal cells are dead and dried out and can form calluses. Trumpet players often get calluses on their lips.

Specialization

Animal bodies are made up of many cells that work together. The body cells are not all the same but are specialized to perform a certain job. Sponges are one of the simplest types of animals, with just four cell types involved in essential processes such as feeding and reproduction. There are more than 200 different types of cells in a human body. The specialized cells contain the basic set of organelles but may develop other features like flagella or cilia.

Sponges are filter feeders that draw water though their funnel-shaped bodies.

DID YOU KNOW? A bird's egg is a single cell. The ostrich egg, at 13 cm (5 inches) long, is the biggest animal cell in the world.

Italian microbiologist Camillo Golgi made many discoveries about animal cells, especially the shape and structure of nerve cells. The Golgi apparatus, an organelle in every complex cell, is named after him. He discovered faint traces of this organelle in the 1890s, but it was not fully described until the 1950s.

The cell nucleus shows up well, but smaller organelles are harder to see without a more powerful electron microscope.

The soft lining of the cheeks is covered in a loose layer of cells. These can be collected easily and viewed under the microscope.

Bacterial Cell

Bacteria have a much smaller and simpler cell than more complex organisms such as animals and plants. The most obvious difference is that there is no nucleus. Instead, the cell's DNA is floating in a rough bundle. Along with those of archaea, the bacterial cell is termed prokaryotic.

Types of Bacteria

There are two main shapes for bacterial cells. A rounded cell is called a coccus, while a rod-shaped bacterium is called a bacillus. When the bacteria form into long chains, they are called streptococci or streptobacilli. Cocci bacteria also form in clusters that are known as staphylococci. A pair of joined round bacteria are called diplococci. Less common cell shapes are bean shapes, comma shapes, long and thin filaments, and spirals.

There are about 30 trillion cells in the human body and about the same number of bacterial cells living on your skin and in your stomach.

The names used to describe bacteria depend a lot on how the cells appear under the microscope. Another important way to identify different bacteria types is to use dyes that target certain chemicals in the cell.

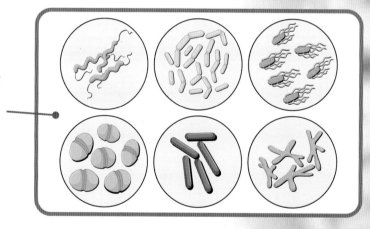

HALL OF FAME:
Alice Catherine Evans
1881–1975

Alice Catherine Evans was an American expert in bacteria. She worked for the United States government, studying disease spread in milk and cheese. Her work helped make these foods much safer. Evans also discovered which bacteria caused dangerous infections of the skin and blood in the 1940s, around the same time the first antibiotic medicines were being developed.

DID YOU KNOW? There are bacteria that eat rock. Some are found living 3 km (1.8 miles) underground and use the chemicals in the rock to provide energy.

Cell Features

All the life processes of the bacteria happen in the cytoplasm, which is a complex mixture of chemicals. The only obvious internal feature is the bundle of DNA. A membrane surrounds the cell, and it may include long taillike flagella or shorter extensions called pili. A cell wall surrounds the membrane, and in some cases the whole cell is inside a protective capsule.

DNA

Cell membrane

Pilus

Capsule

Cell wall

Flagellum

Cytoplasm

The cell wall of a bacterium is made mostly from a complex sugar–based chemical called murein.

Yogurt is a food full of healthy bacteria. Bacteria can cause diseases, but they also help our digestion in many ways, breaking down foods that our stomach chemicals cannot.

Cell Membranes and Transport

Every cell is surrounded by a thin outer layer, or membrane. The membrane is made from fatty chemicals that form a barrier for large molecules, while smaller ones, like water and oxygen, can pass through. Cells rely largely on a physical process called diffusion, where substances naturally spread out from where they are common to where they are rare. However, some cells also use more active systems to move materials around.

Water is pulled into plants by osmosis. If there is not enough water in the plant cells, the cells become soft, and the plant body will wilt.

In and Out of Cells

A cell can release large quantities of a substance using a process called exocytosis. The substance is discharged by the Golgi apparatus into vesicles, or small membrane bags. The vesicle merges with the cell membrane, and the contents are outside the cell. Cells that secrete hormones or enzymes use exocytosis. Endocytosis is the process run in reverse, where material outside the cell is captured in a hollow section of the cell membrane, which then breaks off to form a vesicle inside the cell.

Endocytosis is used by cells that consume nutrients floating in the surrounding waters or that eat smaller cells.

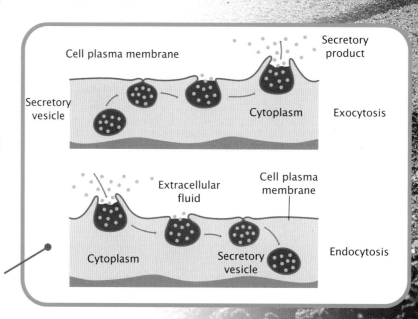

Cell plasma membrane — Secretory product — Secretory vesicle — Cytoplasm — Exocytosis

Extracellular fluid — Cell plasma membrane — Cytoplasm — Secretory vesicle — Endocytosis

DID YOU KNOW? Goblet cells secrete slimy mucus to coat the inside of the nose, lungs, and throat. In an adult human, they produce 1.5 liters (0.3 gallons) every day!

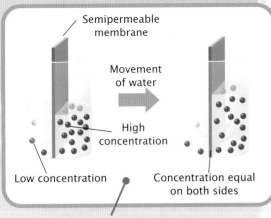

Semipermeable membrane

Movement of water

High concentration

Low concentration

Concentration equal on both sides

Water moves to make the concentration equal on both sides of the membrane.

Osmosis

Cells rely on a special kind of diffusion called osmosis to move water in and out of the cell. Water can cross the membrane, but other chemicals mixed into it cannot. As a result, when there is a high concentration of chemicals dissolved in the cytoplasm, water will diffuse in from outside to dilute it. In the same way, if the cell is in water that is more concentrated than the cytoplasm, osmosis will push water out of the cell, making it dry out.

Water is the universal solvent. This means that it is inside every cell, and all the chemicals needed for life are mixed into it.

HALL OF FAME: Jean–Antoine Nollet
1700–1770

It would be impossible to understand how cells and living things worked without knowing about osmosis. It was discovered in 1748 by Jean–Antoine Nollet, a French priest, who put pure alcohol in a sealed pig's bladder that had been immersed in water. Several hours later, the bladder was bulging with water under great pressure. Osmosis had pushed water inside to dilute the alcohol.

Building Blocks

Cells and all living bodies are constructed from three main types of chemicals: carbohydrates, proteins, and fats. The carbohydrates are an easy source of energy, fats are used as a long-term energy store and in membranes, and whole proteins are hard-working molecules that carry out life processes.

The rigid and strong parts of a plant, such as the trunk of a tree, are made of cellulose. This is a complex carbohydrate that is used in the cell walls of all plants.

Fat and Oils

Fat and oils, also called lipids, are produced by all life-forms. Animal fats tend to be waxy solids that hold more energy than plant fats, which are usually runny oils. A lipid molecule is constructed from three long acid molecules connected together. In solid fats, these molecules are highly tangled, while in an oil, the molecules are able to slip past each other.

Fried foods are cooked in hot oils. A fillet of fish and other animal muscle is a major source of protein. Fried potatoes are a source of carbohydrates.

Many of the chemicals used by life, like the ones in wood, are polymers. This means that they are constructed from chains of smaller molecules linked together.

HALL OF FAME:
Marie Maynard Daly
1921–2003

Marie Maynard Daly was the first Black American woman to be awarded a PhD in chemistry. Daly went on to study the biochemistry of the cell and made discoveries about histones, which are proteins used to store DNA in the nucleus, and cholesterol, which is a type of fat chemical widely used in the body. Daly showed that too much cholesterol was bad for the health.

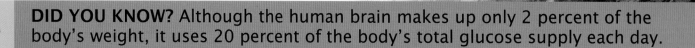

DID YOU KNOW? Although the human brain makes up only 2 percent of the body's weight, it uses 20 percent of the body's total glucose supply each day.

Carbohydrates

The word "carbohydrate" is a combination of "carbon" and "hydrate," which suggests these chemicals seem to be made from water and carbon. It is a little more complicated than that, but carbohydrate molecules generally have equal numbers of carbon and oxygen atoms and about double that of hydrogen atoms. This formula works for molecules of all sizes. Simple carbohydrates with small molecules, like glucose and fructose, are called sugars. They taste sweet and are used as fuel for respiration. Starch is a complex carbohydrate made by chaining smaller glucose molecules together.

Honey is a thick, syrupy mixture of fructose, glucose, and water. Bees make it by dehydrating nectar.

The trunk has light and dark rings. The lighter rings are wider and show where plant cells have been growing fast during the bright summer. Dark rings show slow winter growth.

Cellulose is a polymer made from glucose, as is starch. However, the glucose molecules are arranged differently, so starch is a soft bloblike polymer used as an energy store, while cellulose forms tough strands used to construct the plant's body.

Enzymes

The chemical reactions that take place in a living cell are called metabolism, and most of these reactions are regulated by enzymes. An enzyme is a biological catalyst, which means it is a chemical that allows a reaction to take place that would not happen by itself. There are many thousands of enzymes working in human cells.

Complex Shape

All enzymes are proteins, which are highly complex polymers, and each one has a uniquely intricate shape. Every enzyme has a specific job to do in metabolism, and that job is defined by the shape of the molecule. Its shape allows the enzyme to connect with other chemicals so they can react in some way. This idea is called the lock and key theory.

Fermented foods like pickled vegetables are made by enzymes released by yeasts or bacteria. The enzymes convert the sugars in the foods into acids, such as lactic acid or vinegars.

Protein molecules are made from two or three smaller polymers twisted around each other. The polymers are chains of smaller units called amino acids.

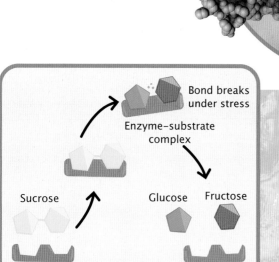

Bond breaks under stress

Enzyme–substrate complex

Sucrose

Glucose   Fructose

Enzyme

This enzyme is splitting a sucrose molecule into simple sugars. The enzyme is not used up in the process.

Lock and Key

In the lock and key theory, an enzyme has a region called the active site that is shaped exactly right for other molecules (called the substrate) to fit into—like a key in a lock. Once connected to the enzymes, the bonds inside the substrate molecules change in strength, so the atoms can rearrange in some way to create a new set of molecules called the products. The products are released from the enzyme, which is then ready to start again.

The shape of an enzyme, or any other protein, is determined by hundreds of smaller units called amino acids. These are chained together in a very particular order and will push and pull on each other to fold up into the final protein shape. No human could figure out how to predict the shape of a protein from the order of its amino acids. However, in 2021, an artificial intelligence made by Google called AlphaFold was able to figure this out. Thanks to AlphaFold, it is now easier to read genes, and artificial enzymes can be designed for use as medicines.

Fermented foods taste sour and acidic due to the action of enzymes.

The large amount of acid in the fermented foods keeps other microscopic organisms from growing on the foods, so they do not rot or go bad very quickly.

DID YOU KNOW? There are over one million chemical reactions happening inside each of your cells every single second, and nearly every one requires an enzyme.

Cell Locomotion

The cells of animals, protists, and some plants and fungi are not always still. They have a way of getting around called cell locomotion. Cell locomotion is used by cells to travel through water or over surfaces. Some cells are built for moving around the body. Others use their locomotion to create a current that pulls material toward them.

Flagella and Cilia

A common method of cell locomotion is to use extensions called flagella or cilia. Their motion creates a thrust force that pushes the cell along. The extensions move because of bundles of proteins inside that slide back and forth, making the cilia and flagella bend and twist. Flagella are long whiplike extensions, while cilia are shorter and generally work together in large groups.

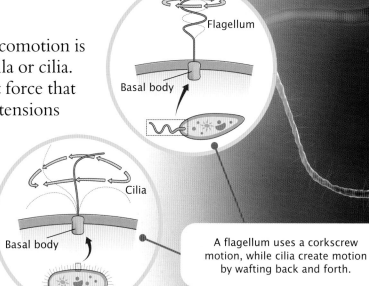

Flagellum

Basal body

Cilia

Basal body

A flagellum uses a corkscrew motion, while cilia create motion by wafting back and forth.

Amoeboid Motion

Cells without flagella or cilia move by extending the cell membrane into footlike appendages called pseudopodia. The pseudopodia shift forward, and the rest of the cell's contents flows into them, so the whole cell has moved. This is how amoebas move, so the motion is called amoeboid. It is not only amoebas that can move like this—white blood cells that defend the body from infection can move like this to attack germs.

Pseudopodia spread out in all directions, and then the cell will choose which one to flow into and move in that direction.

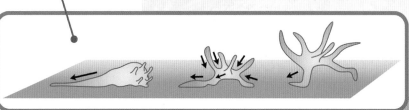

DID YOU KNOW? The lungs and windpipe are lined with ciliated cells, which waft along a blanket of mucus that clears away dust and dirt that gets into the airways.

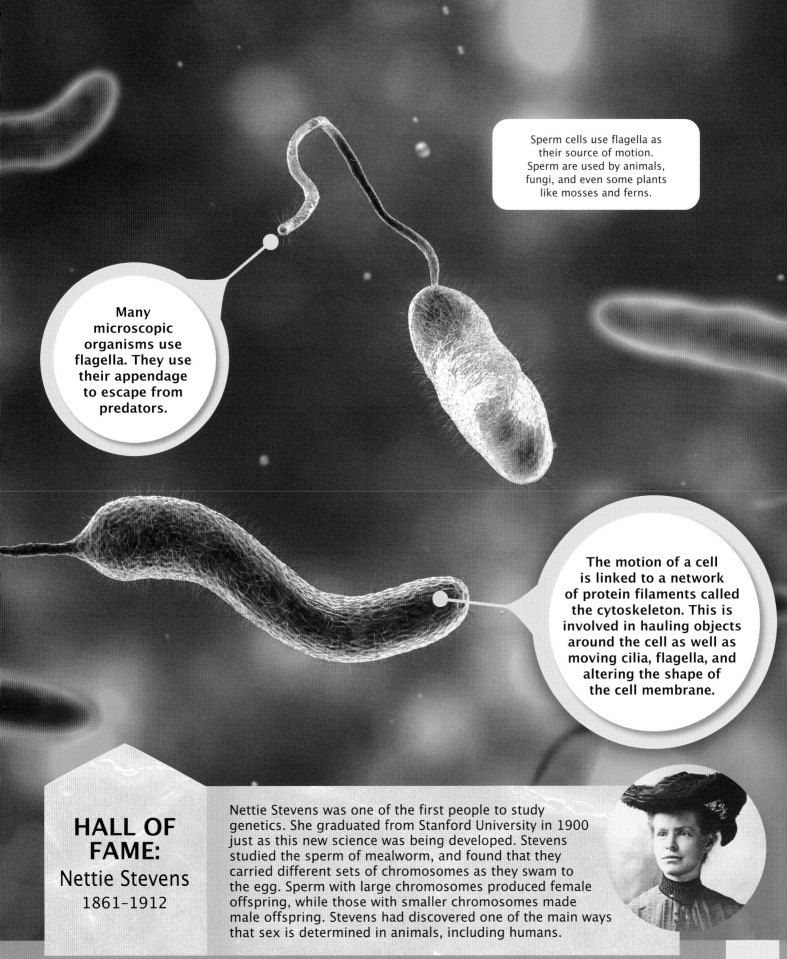

Sperm cells use flagella as their source of motion. Sperm are used by animals, fungi, and even some plants like mosses and ferns.

Many microscopic organisms use flagella. They use their appendage to escape from predators.

The motion of a cell is linked to a network of protein filaments called the cytoskeleton. This is involved in hauling objects around the cell as well as moving cilia, flagella, and altering the shape of the cell membrane.

HALL OF FAME:
Nettie Stevens
1861–1912

Nettie Stevens was one of the first people to study genetics. She graduated from Stanford University in 1900 just as this new science was being developed. Stevens studied the sperm of mealworm, and found that they carried different sets of chromosomes as they swam to the egg. Sperm with large chromosomes produced female offspring, while those with smaller chromosomes made male offspring. Stevens had discovered one of the main ways that sex is determined in animals, including humans.

Cell Division

Cells can grow larger but will soon reach maximum size. For a body to grow, its cells need to divide in two—again and again. The cell division process used for growth like this is called mitosis. It transforms one parent cell into two almost identical offspring cells. Complex cells like those of plants and animals undergo mitosis. Bacteria use a similar system called binary fission.

Fast Growers

Cell division allows single-celled organisms to reproduce very quickly. For example, the microscopic algae that float in seawater as plankton can double in number every 24 hours. Soon there are so many that the invisible plantlike organisms have turned the water green. This explosion of life is called an algal bloom. It can cause problems by spreading poisons in the water and blocking light from reaching the water lower down.

Algal blooms are often caused by fertilizer chemicals from farms washing into water. The chemicals make the algae grow and divide much faster than normal.

Between cell divisions, the cell is in interphase. During this time, the cell grows larger and organizes its chromosomes, ready for the next division.

Mitosis

There are several phases to a cell division by mitosis that ensure the offspring cells always have the same genes as the parent cell. The chromosomes in the nucleus are copied into double versions with an X shape. These are lined up in the middle of the cell, and then each equal half is pulled to opposite ends. Finally, a new cell membrane forms across the middle, and the cell splits into two.

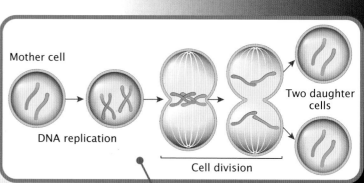

Mother cell

DNA replication

Two daughter cells

Cell division

Each set of chromosomes is pulled to one end of the cell by microfilaments anchored there, separating the two sets. The organelles are divided equally between the two halves.

Matthias Jacob Schleiden was one of the scientists behind cell theory. He had started work as a lawyer, but this made him unhappy—so he switched to studying the new field of cell biology. He was interested in cell division and showed that the contents of the nucleus were always shared by the new cells. He was also interested in evolution and was one of the first biologists to accept Charles Darwin's theory of evolution in 1859.

In the final stage of cell division, known as cytokinesis, a new membrane forms in the middle of the cell dividing up the cytoplasm.

Once the division is complete, a new nucleus forms around the chromosomes in the cell.

DID YOU KNOW? A bacterium can divide in two every 20 minutes. In just 7 hours, one bacteria can grow into more than 2 million.

Symbiogenesis

The theory of symbiogenesis is the idea that the complex cells of multicellular organisms, including humans, evolved many millions of years ago from groups of bacteria that began to work as a team. Bacterial cells are called prokaryotic because they have cells without a nucleus or other obvious organelles. All other life, from single-celled protists to giant trees and whales, have eukaryotic cells with a nucleus and several different organelles.

Symbiogenesis is thought to have happened in a primordial soup, where simple life-forms were crowded together. This is what life was like for most of the history of Earth.

Animallike Cell

The first eukaryotic cells evolved more than 2 billion years ago. It would have been an animallike protist that survived by eating food. First, an archaeon cell grew larger and developed a folded cell membrane, so it had more outer surface to collect foods and nutrients. Some of these folded membranes became trapped in the cell and formed a nucleus. Next, a bacterium was eaten by the cell. However, instead of being destroyed, the incomer started to provide energy to the cell. It was the first mitochondrion.

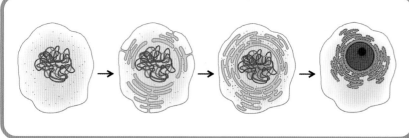

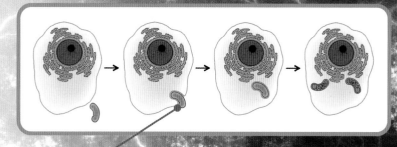

Mitochondria, shown in red, have their own DNA that links them to a large group of bacteria that live in the oceans today. A cell's mitochondria also divide in two, just like bacteria.

HALL OF FAME: Lynn Margulis 1938–2011

Lynn Margulis was the leading researcher in the theory of endosymbiosis. She was a high-flying student in school, and by the age of 20 was already a professional scientist specializing in genetics. Margulis came up with her theory in 1966 but struggled for many years to get other scientists to take it seriously. Today, her theory is accepted as how complex life evolved on Earth.

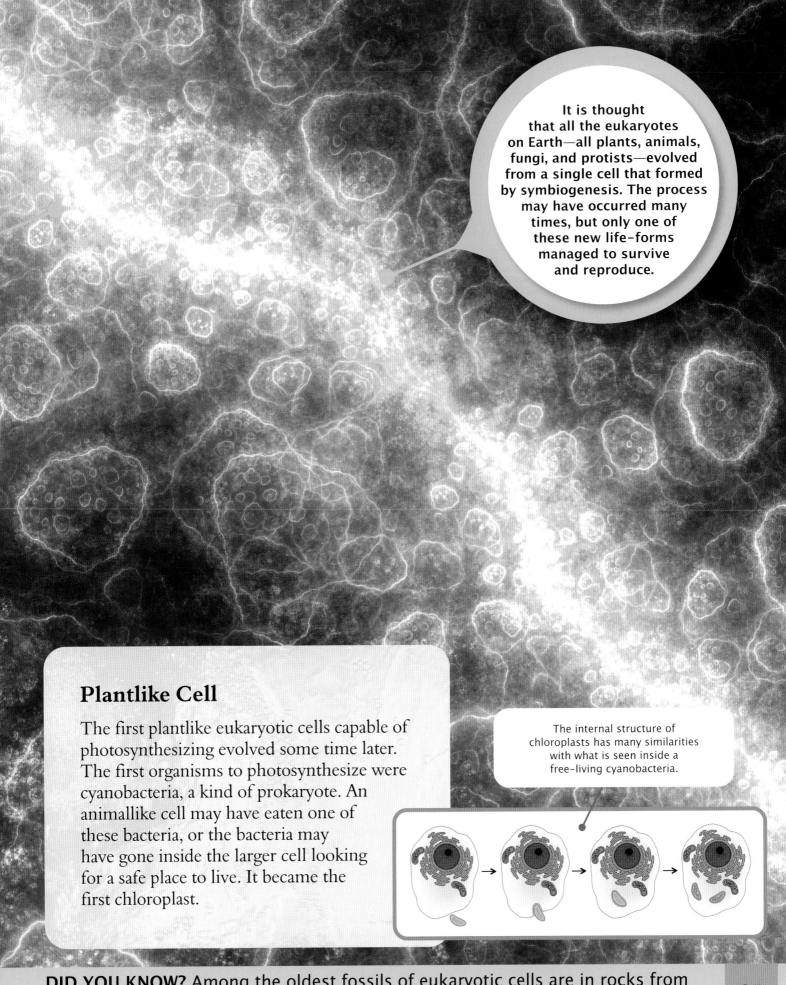

It is thought that all the eukaryotes on Earth—all plants, animals, fungi, and protists—evolved from a single cell that formed by symbiogenesis. The process may have occurred many times, but only one of these new life-forms managed to survive and reproduce.

Plantlike Cell

The first plantlike eukaryotic cells capable of photosynthesizing evolved some time later. The first organisms to photosynthesize were cyanobacteria, a kind of prokaryote. An animallike cell may have eaten one of these bacteria, or the bacteria may have gone inside the larger cell looking for a safe place to live. It became the first chloroplast.

The internal structure of chloroplasts has many similarities with what is seen inside a free-living cyanobacteria.

DID YOU KNOW? Among the oldest fossils of eukaryotic cells are in rocks from India that are about 1.6 billion years old.

Viruses

A virus is a biologically active entity, but it is not alive. It is not made from a cell but is built from a piece of DNA (or RNA) wrapped up in a coat made of proteins. The viral DNA is parasitic, and it takes over the machinery of cells to make copies of itself.

A coronavirus is named after the way it is covered in "spike" proteins. When viewed through a microscope, they look like a crown, or corona, around the outside.

Viral Diseases

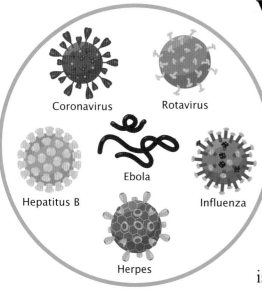

Coronavirus   Rotavirus

Ebola

Hepatitus B   Influenza

Herpes

Viruses are organized by their distinctive shapes. All viruses cause diseases in a target organism. Most viruses are harmless to humans, but we still have several viral diseases. Influenza, or flu, is a viral disease. Herpes viruses create several diseases, including chickenpox. Ebola virus is a rare but dangerous infection, while rotavirus attacks the stomach and hepatitis viruses damage the liver. Covid is caused by a type of coronavirus.

Infection

A virus is able to bond to its target cell using its protein coat. It then injects its DNA into the cell. The DNA takes over the cell's system for copying its own DNA and makes many copies of itself. The viral DNA's genes carry the instructions for making its coating proteins, and the cell is used to manufacture those. Eventually, the cell is so full of new viruses that it bursts. The viruses then infect the next cell.

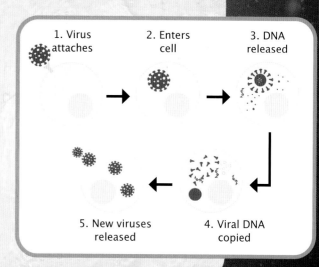

1. Virus attaches   2. Enters cell   3. DNA released

5. New viruses released   4. Viral DNA copied

DID YOU KNOW? The viruses that cause the common cold are only 20 nanometers across. That means that 50,000 of them could line up on a pinhead.

The immune system learns to recognize each new virus from the shapes on its surface. If this virus enters the body again, the immune system will tackle it more quickly than the first infection.

The spike proteins are shaped to lock onto something on the outside of a particular target cell. This is why certain viruses attack the throat and nose, and others might infect the stomach.

HALL OF FAME:
Martinus Beijerinck

1851–1931

Dutch microbiologist Martinus Beijerinck discovered viruses in 1898. He was working with viruses that attack plants and found that these disease-causing agents were smaller than bacteria, the smallest life-forms known. Beijerinck suggested the name virus and described it as a nonliving object somewhere between a molecule and a cell.

DNA and Chromosomes

DNA, short for deoxyribonucleic acid, is a chemical stored inside the nucleus of a cell on structures called chromosomes. It carries the organism's genes, which are coded instructions on how to build a new cell and grow an entire body.

A human cell has 46 chromosomes, but that number varies a lot from species to species. Half of the chromosomes come from each of the parents.

Chromosomes

DNA is quite a delicate substance. It is protected inside the cell's nucleus, where it is kept separate from other chemicals that might damage it and alter its genetic coding. The long strands are coiled up to make bundles called chromosomes. The DNA is only uncoiled when it is being copied and decoded. The chromosome is mostly coiled and compact during cell division. The rest of the time, it thins out into finer strands.

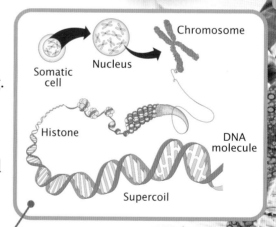

Somatic cell

Nucleus

Chromosome

Histone

DNA molecule

Supercoil

The DNA strands are coiled around support proteins called histones, and then these coils are coiled and coiled many times to make a compact "supercoil."

HALL OF FAME:
Rosalind Franklin
1920–1958

Rosalind Franklin was a chemist who used X-rays to figure out the structure of molecules. DNA had been discovered in the 1860s, but 90 years later no one knew its shape. Franklin's X-ray photographs offered the first clue that the molecule was a helix (a shape like a spiral ladder). This was the big breakthrough that allowed other scientists to figure out how DNA works.

DID YOU KNOW? If all the DNA in your body was uncoiled, it would stretch from the Earth to the Sun and back 20 times!

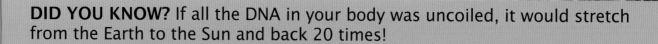

DNA Structure

Deoxyribonucleic acid is a polymer built from several units to make a twisted ladder shape or helix. Ribose sugar forms the sides. There are four nucleic acids that connect in pairs to form the "rungs." The order of these acids along the DNA strand spells out a four-letter code. Genes are written in this code.

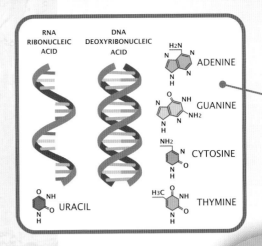

The four nucleic acids in DNA are simplified to the letters A, G, C, and T. RNA, or ribonucleic acid, is constructed from a single nucleic acid strand and uses the acid U instead of T.

The parental genes are altered and shuffled into new combinations for the offspring. This is how children inherit the features of their parents.

A full set of chromosomes is called a karyotype. Each chromosome is part of a pair, with one each coming from the mother and father. Humans have 23 pairs.

Reading Genes

Genes are a chemical code stored in the DNA. The code is made of a string of four nucleic acids: T, C, G, and A. The order of these acids in each gene gives the recipe for making a particular protein, such as those used as enzymes or in muscles.

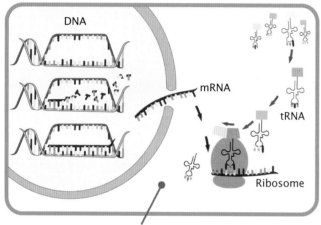

The ribosome constructs a protein by chaining amino acids together in the order set out by the gene.

Copy and Translate

The DNA code in the nucleus is copied onto a strand of messenger RNA (mRNA), which then leaves the nucleus and heads to a ribosome—the cell's protein-building factory. The ribosome translates the genetic code into a protein. It does this with transfer RNA (tRNA) molecules. Each tRNA fits with a specific three-letter sequence on the mRNA, and that sequence relates to one amino acid. The tRNAs read the sequences in the gene to create a chain of amino acids in the right order.

Sequence and Structure

At its simplest, the genetic code is a list of amino acids that show the order in which these small units must be arranged to make useful proteins. There are around 20 amino acids used in nature, and proteins can have several hundred of them. This means there are vast numbers of possible proteins, but only the ones coded in genes work in the body. The DNA molecule is able to store these correct codes and pass them on without introducing mistakes.

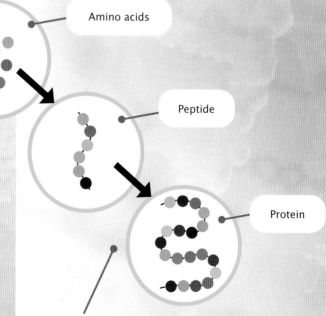

A protein is a polymer made from long chains of amino acids. A single chain of amino acids is called a peptide, and a protein molecule has two or three peptides.

DID YOU KNOW? Human DNA carries a code made of 3 billion characters. This entire code is copied when a cell divides, which happens 2 trillion times every day in your body.

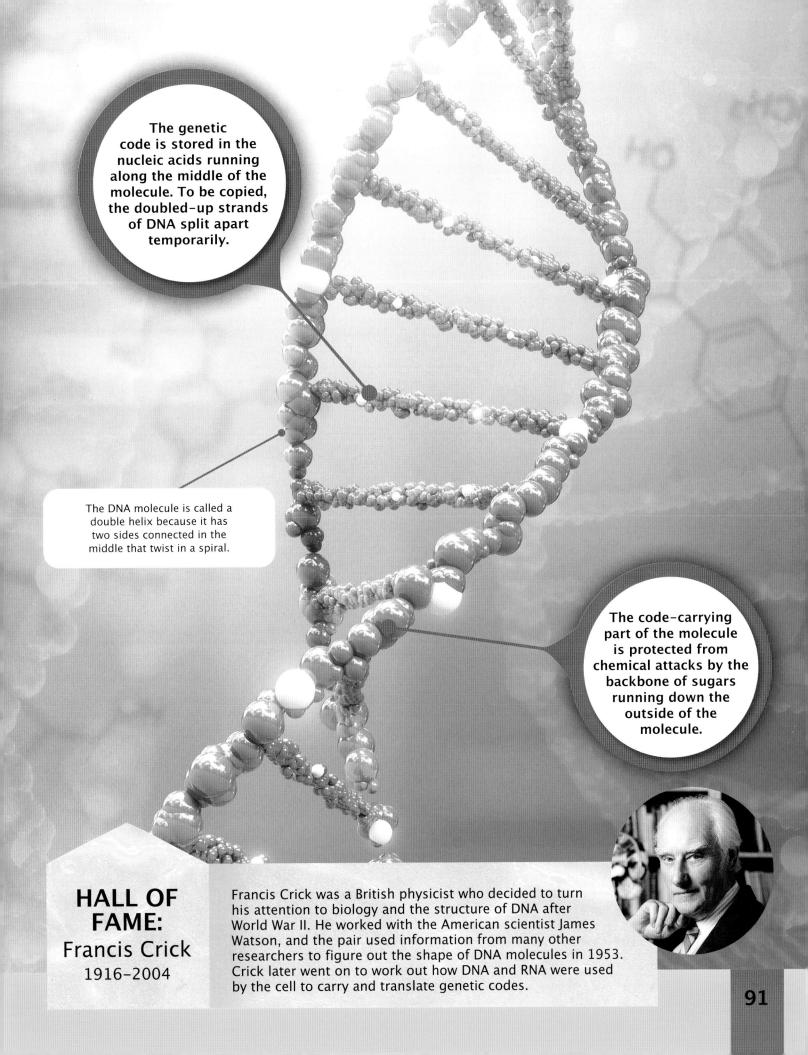

The genetic code is stored in the nucleic acids running along the middle of the molecule. To be copied, the doubled-up strands of DNA split apart temporarily.

The DNA molecule is called a double helix because it has two sides connected in the middle that twist in a spiral.

The code-carrying part of the molecule is protected from chemical attacks by the backbone of sugars running down the outside of the molecule.

HALL OF FAME:
Francis Crick
1916–2004

Francis Crick was a British physicist who decided to turn his attention to biology and the structure of DNA after World War II. He worked with the American scientist James Watson, and the pair used information from many other researchers to figure out the shape of DNA molecules in 1953. Crick later went on to work out how DNA and RNA were used by the cell to carry and translate genetic codes.

Genotypes and Phenotypes

There are two ways of understanding genes. The genotype is a record of what chemical codes a person has in their cells. The phenotype is a record of a body characteristic, such as hair color, which is inherited from the parents. A big part of the study of genetics is figuring out how genotypes are linked to phenotypes.

Family members look similar because they have inherited a set of genes from both parents. Often a grandchild has the same recessive phenotype as a grandparent—something not seen in either of their parents.

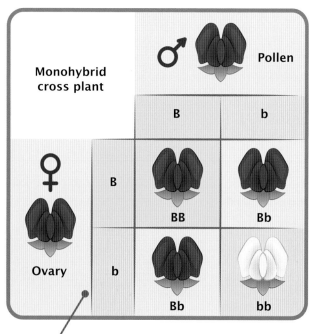

When both parents have the dominant (B) and recessive (b) genes, three-quarters of the offspring will have the dominant phenotype, while a quarter will be recessive.

Dominance

A genotype always contains two copies of the same gene—one from each parent. In many cases, the phenotype created is controlled by which version of the genes is dominant. A dominant version will always create the phenotype if it is present. A nondominant, or recessive, version of the gene is only seen if the genotype contains two copies of this version.

The many different kinds of cat fur are controlled by a few codominant genes.

Codominance

For some genes, the different versions are not dominant over one of the other. Instead if the genotype has a mix of versions, their effects are merged together to make a phenotype that is halfway between the two characteristics. This system is called codominance.

HALL OF FAME:
Gregor Mendel
1822–1884

Gregor Mendel was a German-speaking monk living in what is now the Czech Republic. He spent several years carefully studying how it was that different characterics (what we now call phenotypes) of pea plants were passed on generation after generation. Mendel knew nothing about DNA (it had not even been discovered yet), but his discoveries about dominance and codominance became the foundations of the science of genetics.

Black is the dominant version of the hair color gene. If people inherit that version of the gene, they will always have black hair.

A child shares half of the same genes with each of its parents and a quarter of the same genes with each grandparent.

DID YOU KNOW? The human genome (total collection of DNA) has around 20,000 genes. About 98 percent of the DNA in a cell carries no genetic code at all.

Meiosis

A special kind of cell division, called meiosis, is needed for sexual reproduction. Meiosis makes cells with a half set of genes—these are called sex cells. Two sex cells can merge to make a full set of genes for a new individual. This method of breeding is called sexual reproduction, and it ensures that each child has a highly varied set of genes.

The four offspring cells created by meiosis can be used as sex cells, either sperm and eggs, in reproduction. Often only one of the four makes it to this stage.

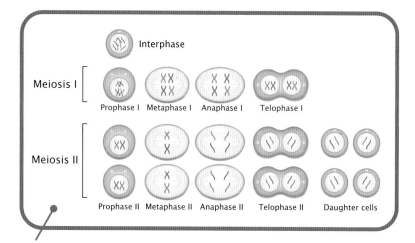

The starting cell is described as diploid, because it has a full set of paired up chromosomes inherited from two parents. The daughter cells made by meiosis are haploid, meaning they have just one of each of the pairs of chromosomes.

Steps

Meiosis is two cell divisions in one. The first division organizes the chromosomes into their pairs and then draws one of each pair to opposite ends of the cell. The cell then divides in two and creates daughter cells with a half set of chromosomes. The next division is more like mitosis (see page 82), and the two half-set cells divide again to make a total of four daughter cells.

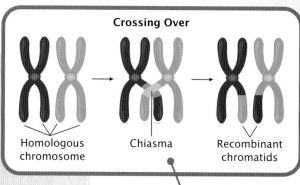

The chromosomes have an X-shape because they have been duplicated ready for cell division. They have two identical copies connected in the middle. During crossing over, only one of these halves swaps DNA.

Crossing Over

Unlike in mitosis, where the daughter cells always have identical genes, meiosis is deliberately mixing chromosomes up to make four daughter cells with a unique set of DNA. One of the ways this is done is called recombination, or crossing over. During the first division in meiosis, the paired up chromosomes are lined up next to each other. They are so close that they can tangle up and swap chunks of DNA.

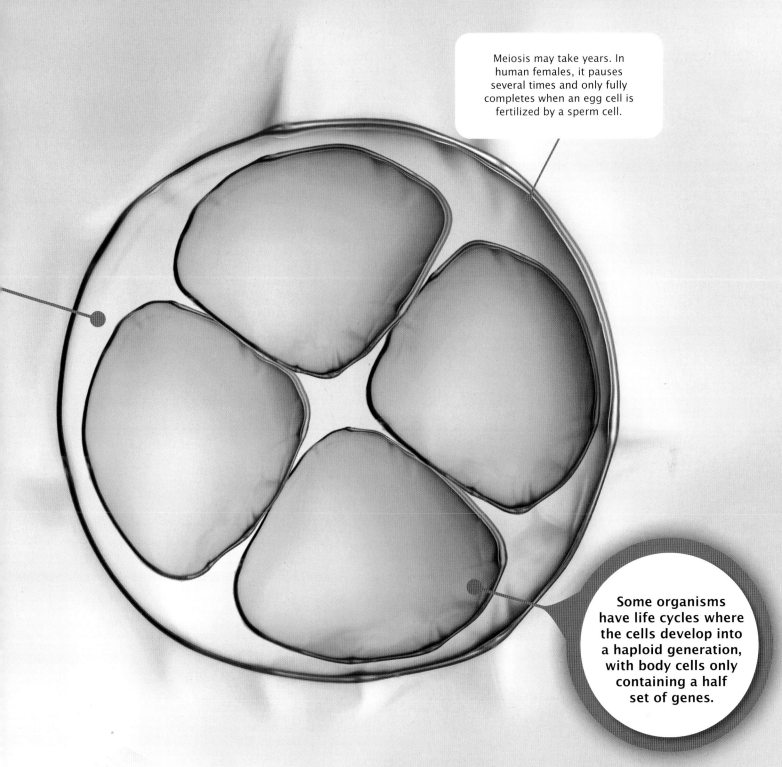

Meiosis may take years. In human females, it pauses several times and only fully completes when an egg cell is fertilized by a sperm cell.

Some organisms have life cycles where the cells develop into a haploid generation, with body cells only containing a half set of genes.

HALL OF FAME:
Barbara McClintock
1902–1992

Starting out as a botanist studying crops grown on American farms, Barbara McClintock discovered recombination, one of the most important phenomena in genetics. She made this breakthrough while studying the chromosomes of maize, observing that they were muddled up during meiosis. Later, McClintock also made breakthroughs on how genes were read and expressed as phenotypes.

DID YOU KNOW? A female oceanic sunfish, or Mola mola, produces 300 million eggs each breeding season, which is the most for any vertebrate.

Sex Cells and Fertilization

Most multicellular organisms reproduce sexually. This involves two types of sex cells, or gametes, fusing together in a process called fertilization. The female gamete is the egg, and the male one is the sperm. Together they make a zygote, which is the first cell of a new individual.

The human sperm is only 0.005 mm (0.0002 in) wide. The human egg is 20 times bigger, and at 0.1 mm (0.004 in) across, it is just about visible with the naked eye.

Gametes

Sperm and eggs are haploid, which means they only have half a set of chromosomes. The zygote they produce is diploid and has a full set. The sperm is built for swimming and has a long flagellum. It carries only energy supplies and DNA. The egg is much larger and cannot move itself. As well as some DNA, the egg contains everything else the new zygote will need to begin its life.

Egg

Sperm

HALL OF FAME:
Oscar Hertwig
1849–1922

In 1876, German zoologist Oscar Hertwig discovered the process of fertilization by watching through a microscope as the sperm and egg of sea urchins fused together. Hertwig also discovered the process of meiosis. Additionally, he noticed that the chemicals in the nucleus were passed from cell to cell and must be the way characteristics are inherited. This was true, but it took almost another 100 years to figure out how!

DID YOU KNOW? The average female human releases about 350 ripe eggs in her whole life. An adult male human produces about 100 million sperm every day.

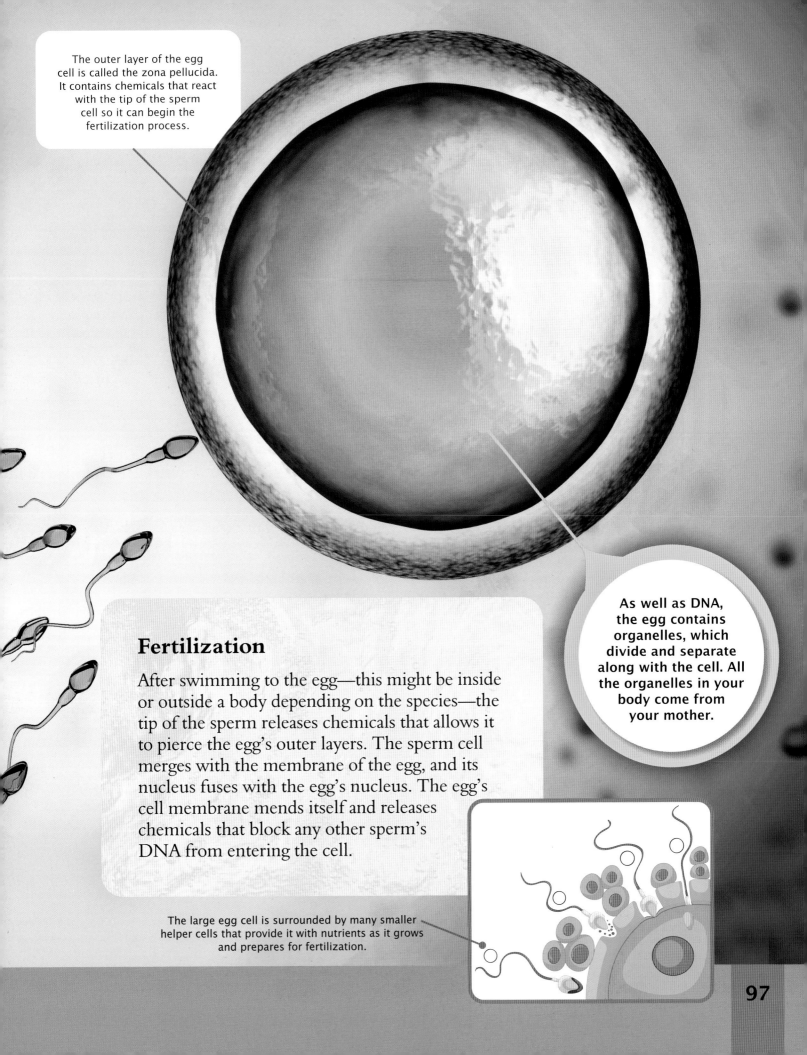

The outer layer of the egg cell is called the zona pellucida. It contains chemicals that react with the tip of the sperm cell so it can begin the fertilization process.

As well as DNA, the egg contains organelles, which divide and separate along with the cell. All the organelles in your body come from your mother.

Fertilization

After swimming to the egg—this might be inside or outside a body depending on the species—the tip of the sperm releases chemicals that allows it to pierce the egg's outer layers. The sperm cell merges with the membrane of the egg, and its nucleus fuses with the egg's nucleus. The egg's cell membrane mends itself and releases chemicals that block any other sperm's DNA from entering the cell.

The large egg cell is surrounded by many smaller helper cells that provide it with nutrients as it grows and prepares for fertilization.

97

Genetic Engineering

Scientists have figured out ways of changing the characteristics of various life-forms by editing their genetic codes. Most often, they engineer simple organisms like bacteria and yeasts, but more complex plants and animals are also being altered. Genetic engineering can be used to make better medicines and cure diseases.

This mouse has been given some genes from a jellyfish that can glow in the dark. The mouse's skin makes the glowing chemicals.

Medical Breakthroughs

Genetic engineering can be used to make medicines and other useful chemicals on a large scale very cheaply. A good example is the way insulin is made to treat diabetes. It is not possible to make pure insulin from raw ingredients in a factory. However, genetic engineers have added the gene for insulin production to a bacterium. The bacterium is grown inside vats, and it produces the complex chemical in large amounts.

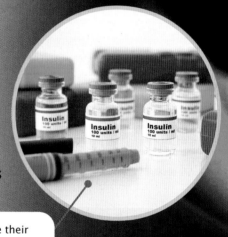

Some diabetic people cannot make their own insulin to control their energy supplies. However, the insulin made by genetic engineering works just as well.

Plants can be engineered to withstand the pesticides that are used to kill weeds or other unwanted plants growing nearby.

GMOs

Genetically modified organisms, or GMOs, are plants and animals that have been created by genetic engineers. GMOs are made for several reasons, but the most important is producing food. Genetically modified crops are able to grow well in places where regular crops could not. However, some scientists worry that the GM plants will breed with wild plants and create dangerous pests and weeds.

The genes added by genetic engineers can be passed on to the next generation just like natural genes. Genetically modified organisms must be carefully controlled so that their added genes do not escape into the wild.

The glowing chemicals could be used to target cancers and other problems in the body so that they can be spotted very early.

HALL OF FAME: Jennifer Doudna 1964–

There are several techniques of editing DNA sequences, but the one used most often today is called CRISPR. This system was developed by Jennifer Doudna along with her collaborator Emmanuelle Charpentier. In 2020, the pair received the Nobel Prize for their work. CRISPR takes a system used by bacterial cells and uses it to add DNA to any sequence of genes.

DID YOU KNOW? Genetically modified goats have been given the genes for spider's silk. The milk from these goats contains large quantities of silk, which is used by scientists for research into this amazing material.

The Theory of Evolution

The organisms that live on Earth today were not always here. Instead they evolved from earlier life-forms that have now become extinct and disappeared. Evolution is a system of change that is driven by a process called natural selection.

This frog has failed to avoid being captured by a predator. Its genes and characteristics will not be passed on to the next generation.

This plesiosaur was a reptile and relative of the dinosaurs. It lived in the oceans around 100 million years ago. It evolved from an older animal that lived on land.

Fossils

We know that different animals and plants lived long ago because of fossils. Fossils are the remains of living things that have turned to stone. They provide a record of how life has evolved slowly over many millions of years.

The fossils also help to show how the environment was changing, and these changes are the major force that drives evolution. Simple life first appeared at least 3.5 billion years ago. All life that exists today—and all the extinct life seen in fossils—evolved from those early life-forms.

HALL OF FAME:
Charles Darwin
1809–1882

English naturalist Charles Darwin is world famous for publishing his book *On the Origin of Species* in 1859, in which he set out his theory of evolution by natural selection. At the time, many people were shocked by Darwin's ideas, but many years of research show that the theory is definitely the way life is able to change gradually to adapt to new habitats and conditions.

Natural Selection

All living things compete with each other for food and living space to survive. This struggle drives evolution using a process called natural selection. No group of organisms is identical; there is always variation. Some are a better fit for surviving in their habitat. These "fit" individuals do well and have many offspring, which are also "fit." Organisms that are less well suited for their habitat die without reproducing. This means that useful characteristics gradually spread through a population—and so species evolve slowly over time. The history of life is made of many tiny steps of evolution like this. Over billions of years, they have created the wealth of life on Earth.

The theory of evolution by natural selection was thought up by Charles Darwin as he traveled the world on HMS *Beagle*. On his voyage, he saw many unusual animals and plants.

The genes that this heron has inherited mean that it is a successful hunter— today at least. The better it is at hunting, the more likely it is to pass on those "fit" genes to the next generation.

Webbed feet are a useful characteristic for animals that swim. The frogs that live on land have evolved toes without webs.

DID YOU KNOW? Charles Darwin probably got many of his ideas about how life-forms were all related to each other from his grandfather Erasmus Darwin, who also wrote about evolution.

How New Species Arise

A species is a group of organisms that look similar and live in the same way—and, most importantly, can breed with each other to produce the next generation. Every species that is living today evolved from an older one that is now extinct. Closely related species all evolved from the same common ancestor.

The savannahs of Africa have a lot of room for large animals and many opportunities for different species to live in their own way.

Adaptive Radiation

New species form from common ancestors because natural selection allows different groups to adapt to changing conditions. This leads to adaptive radiation, where related species take on different characteristics to survive in different ways. A good example are Darwin's finches living in the Galapagos Islands. They all evolved from the same ancestor but now have different beak shapes, so they can eat varied foods on the islands.

Birds with chunky beaks eat hard seeds, while more pointed beaks are used for snatching insects.

HALL OF FAME:
Georges Cuvier
1769–1832

Experts in fossils are called paleontologists, and they work to find the long-gone common ancestors of today's species. Georges Cuvier was a leading figure in the early days of fossil science. In the 1790s, he showed that fossils were not just ancient versions of today's animals. Instead, they were different species that had become extinct. This discovery changed the way scientists thought about life on Earth.

DID YOU KNOW? More than 99 percent of all species that have evolved on Earth have now become extinct.

Zebras share a common ancestor with horses and donkeys. Together, this group of horselike species are called the equids.

Speciation

There is more than one way that a new species can diverge from an older one. The most common is called allopatry, where a species becomes divided in two by geography. Natural selection means that they evolve in different ways, and by the time they mix again, these groups have become two species. In sympatry, a new species forms among the older one as some members specialize in targeting a new source of food and diverge from the rest.

In these two examples, one species becomes two. Natural selection can also transform a whole species, so it becomes a new form of life.

There are dozens of different antelope species living in this part of Africa. Each one is adapted to eating a particular kind of food in a particular habitat.

Coevolution

Natural selection changes organisms so that they fit better with the environment around them. This leads to some amazing effects. In coevolution, the survival of two species is so closely linked that they evolve together in some way. In convergent evolution, completely different organisms end up adapting in the same way to their habitats.

Mimicry and Camouflage

Animals evolve disguises that work in their habitat. Camouflage allows the creature to blend in with the colors, tones, and patterns of its surroundings so it cannot be spotted by predators or prey. Mimicry is when an animal evolves to look like another animal. Mimics often pretend to be a more dangerous species to scare off attackers, or groups of poisonous species evolve to look alike so they all benefit from the same warning signal they give to predators.

This gecko is hoping we cannot see it against the bark. Outside of this habitat, this woodland disguise would be useless.

The monarch butterfly is bright orange as a warning to predators that its body is filled with a poison. Several other butterfly species use the same hue to send the same message.

Convergent Evolution

There are multiple examples of how natural selection has come up with the same answers for surviving in a habitat many times over. The best examples are the way animals that live in the sea evolve the same body shape. Dolphins and sharks are distant relatives. Sharks are fish that evolved 450 million years ago and dolphins evolved from land mammals around 50 million years ago, but they both have the same streamlined body.

These two species have evolved similar body shapes. However, the dolphin's tail flukes are horizontal while the shark's tail fins are vertical.

DID YOU KNOW? The world's largest flower, the stinking corpse lily, has evolved to smell of rotting meat instead of a sweet perfume. The scent attracts meat-eating flies that pollinate the strange Indonesian plant.

This flower has evolved to attract butterflies. It has a wide and flat landing area for the insects to stand on while they feed on nectar and collect pollen.

Many flowering plants rely on insects to transfer pollen from one bloom to the next, and so the insects and plants have coevolved.

HALL OF FAME:
Mary Anning
1799–1847

Mary Anning grew up on the southern coast of England near a region of cliffs that are full of fossils. She became a fossil hunter as a child and made some very important discoveries. Perhaps her most famous was the first skeleton of an ichthyosaur in 1811. Ichthyosaurs were marine reptiles, and convergent evolution meant they looked a lot like sharks and dolphins. Anning's other fossil finds inspired other scientists to study extinct animals, and this led to the discovery of the dinosaurs.

Sexual Selection

Natural selection is a process that allows only the organisms best suited to their environment to survive. How does this explain why some animals have features like bright feathers or huge tails, which make it harder for them to survive? The answer is a special kind of evolution called sexual selection.

A male bird of paradise from New Guinea needs to spend a lot of time and energy getting noticed among the dense leaves.

Sexual Dimorphism

There are often obvious differences between the males and females of certain species. Features particular to one sex may be used to signal fitness to members of the other sex. Such features may include anatomical curiosities that have no obvious use for survival, such as colorful tails or huge antlers. The message here seems to be—if I can survive with something this impractical attached to me, I really must be fit.

This male duck is out to impress the female duck, showing off his plumage. She will choose which male bird to mate with this year.

Females that mate with big-headed males like this will produce male offspring that also have wide heads. In this way, the sexually selected feature spreads through the population.

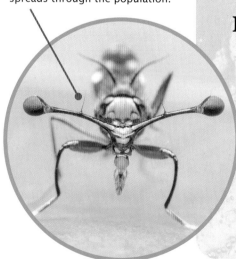

Big Heads

This stalk-eyed fly has a very wide head with bulging eyes on each side. The males uses this feature to figure out which one is in charge and has the right to mate with a female. They line up head to head, and the male with the widest stalks wins. This system prevents risky fights. The loser will leave and look for another mate. Next time, he might be the winner in the same head-to-head competition.

DID YOU KNOW? Deer stags use antlers to signal who is the fittest. The Irish elk is an extinct deer species that had antlers 3.5 m (11.5 ft) wide, about the same length as a hatchback car.

The spiraled tail feathers or streamers catch the eye but also make it harder for the bird to fly. Only the fittest birds can stay strong and healthy despite these unhelpful features.

The bird relies on a courtship display to attract a mate. The females watch the males show off before opting for the best performing mate.

HALL OF FAME:
Richard Dawkins
1941-

Richard Dawkins, a British professor of zoology, is most famous for introducing the public to the ideas of neo-Darwinism, sometimes called the selfish gene. These ideas emerged in the 1960s and seek to explain how everything that happens in evolution is driven by the need for DNA to make copies of itself. Natural selection is really working at the genetic level, and living things are just survival machines built by DNA to help it copy itself.

Ecosystems

Living organisms cannot survive alone. They require a place to live and a source of energy and nutrients. In all the places on Earth where life can survive, there is an ecosystem—a community of living things that rely on each other for survival. Evolution has given organisms the tools to survive in even the harshest environments.

A coral reef is a very diverse ecosystem in warm, shallow ocean waters, filled with shellfish, fish, and corals. Coral reefs are sometimes described as the rain forests of the sea due to the many species found there.

Ecological Factors

The study of ecosystems is called ecology. Ecologists have found that each ecosystem has a unique collection of factors that help or hinder the survival of its members. Biological factors come from other species living in the area. For example, one species may be a source of food, and others may pose problems, such as predation, disease, or competition for living space. The ecosystem also has nonbiological, or abiotic factors, such as weather changes and types of soils.

Ecosystems usually experience different seasons throughout the year, where changes in temperature, day length, and rain levels impact the wildlife.

HALL OF FAME:
Eduard Suess
1831–1914

Ecosystems of different kinds fill all of Earth's living space or biosphere. The term "biosphere" was coined in 1875 by Eduard Suess, an Austrian geologist. The biosphere is the part of the planet from the deep rocks to high atmosphere where life can survive. This made Suess one of the first ecologists. In the 1920s, his ideas were rediscovered by scientists who were trying to understand how wildlife communities worked.

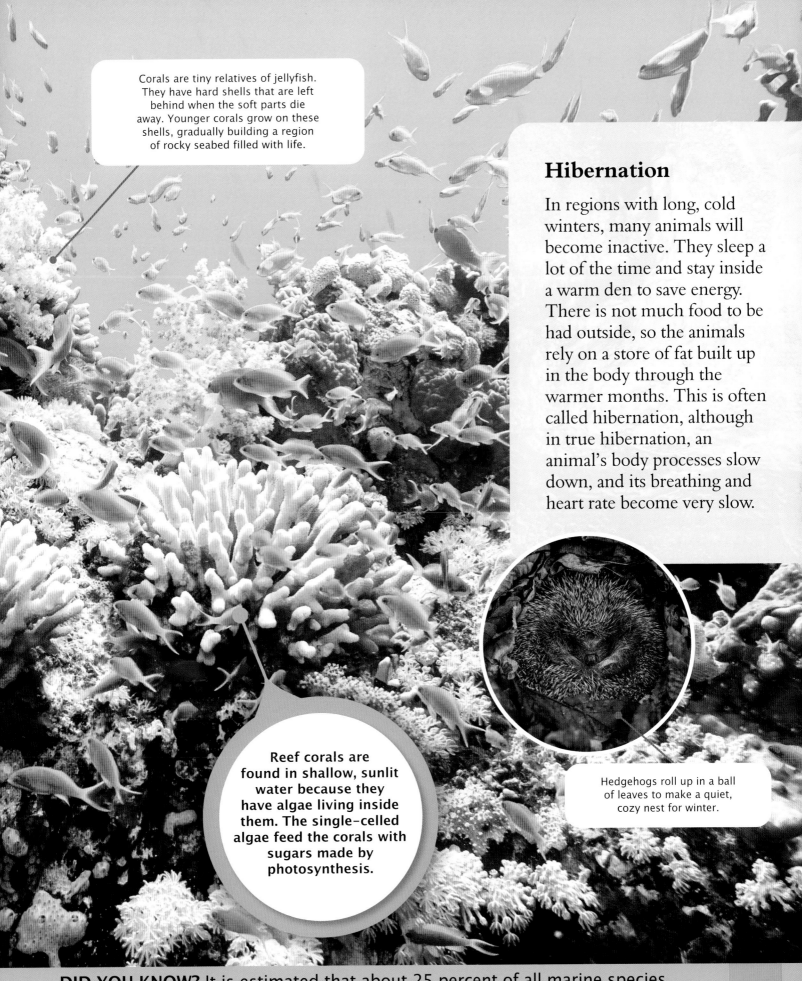

Corals are tiny relatives of jellyfish. They have hard shells that are left behind when the soft parts die away. Younger corals grow on these shells, gradually building a region of rocky seabed filled with life.

Hibernation

In regions with long, cold winters, many animals will become inactive. They sleep a lot of the time and stay inside a warm den to save energy. There is not much food to be had outside, so the animals rely on a store of fat built up in the body through the warmer months. This is often called hibernation, although in true hibernation, an animal's body processes slow down, and its breathing and heart rate become very slow.

Reef corals are found in shallow, sunlit water because they have algae living inside them. The single-celled algae feed the corals with sugars made by photosynthesis.

Hedgehogs roll up in a ball of leaves to make a quiet, cozy nest for winter.

DID YOU KNOW? It is estimated that about 25 percent of all marine species are found in coral reefs.

Food Webs

All living things need energy and nutrients. Plants get theirs by harnessing the energy in sunlight to produce fuel using photosynthesis. Animals get what they need by eating, or consuming, the bodies of plants and other animals. A food web is a set of connections between members of an ecosystem, based on what is eating what.

Interconnected

A food web begins with a producer, which captures a source of energy from the wider environment. In almost all ecosystems, the producers are plants. The producers are eaten by primary consumers, or herbivores (plant-eaters). These animals are then eaten by carnivores (meat-eaters), which are called secondary consumers. Some members of the web eat both plant and animal foods and are called omnivores.

These whales are filterfeeders. They sift out the food from the water through a baleen, which is a fringe of flexible plates around the mouth.

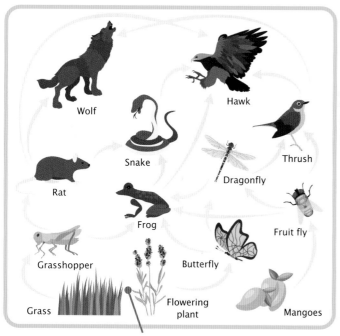

Wolf

Hawk

Snake

Thrush

Dragonfly

Rat

Frog

Fruit fly

Grasshopper

Butterfly

Grass

Flowering plant

Mangoes

The top of the food web is occupied by the "apex predators," such as wolves and birds of prey.

A pod of Bryde's whales are taking gulps of seawater filled with shoals of small fish. The whales are secondary consumers in the ocean food web.

DID YOU KNOW? A food web is also a map of how energy flows through an ecosystem keeping the wildlife alive. Almost all that energy originally comes from the Sun.

An ocean food web is based on phytoplankton, which are tiny, photosynthesizing organisms that float in the water.

Detritivores

Plants rely on a supply of nonliving chemical nutrients in the soil. These are put there by a group of consumers called detritivores, or "waste eaters." Detritivores eat the waste and remains of other living things, turning them back into soil. Fungi are common detritivores, as are bacteria and flies.

A fungus grows on damp, dead wood, slowly digesting it.

HALL OF FAME:
Rachel Carson
1907–1964

Rachel Carson was an American writer and naturalist who introduced the public to environmental problems caused by pollution and habitat destruction. In 1962, she wrote a book called *Silent Spring*, where she warned that the chemicals used on the world's farmland were killing so much wildlife that whole ecosystems would collapse. The sounds of animals, like birdsong in spring, would disappear. Thanks to Carson, governments and scientists began to work harder to protect the environment.

Carbon Cycle

All life is based on carbon chemicals. Fat, sugars, proteins, and vitamins are all made up of complex chains of carbon atoms. All organisms take in and give out carbon all the time, and this creates a flow of carbon through the natural environment. This is called the carbon cycle.

Natural Cycle

Carbon is drawn into the food web by plants and other producers that take carbon dioxide gas out of the air or water and turn it into sugars using photosynthesis. This is where all the carbon chemicals in almost every living thing on Earth come from. Life returns some of this carbon dioxide to the environment through respiration. Some of the carbon in the remains of dead organisms becomes locked away in carbon sinks underground. Sometimes, these carbon sinks form coal and oil.

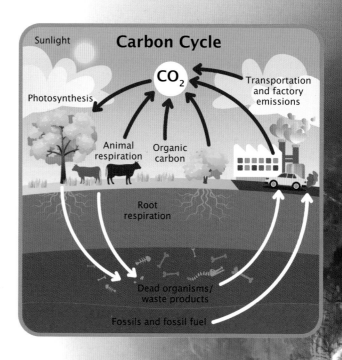

Carbon Cycle

Sunlight
Photosynthesis
CO_2
Transportation and factory emissions
Animal respiration
Organic carbon
Root respiration
Dead organisms/waste products
Fossils and fossil fuel

Climate change is melting the world's ice and glaciers. Life adapted to live in these cold places are running out of habitats.

Disrupted Cycle

In the natural carbon cycle, the amount taken in by life is equal to the amount given back out. However, by burning the coal, gas, and oil stored in carbon sinks—known as fossil fuels—extra carbon is added to the air, disrupting the natural cycle. The extra carbon gases in the air traps heat around the planet, making the world warmer and changing the climate.

DID YOU KNOW? The amount of carbon dioxide in the air today is 50 percent higher than it was in the year 1750—and it is still rising.

Climate change is making some regions warmer and drier. Forests become so dry that they catch fire in devastating wildfires.

It will take many decades for the forests to regrow. It may be that the area is now too dry for trees, so grasslands or deserts will replace the burned forest.

Forest wood is an important store of carbon. Wildfires burn the wood and add more carbon dioxide into the air. This makes climate change even worse.

HALL OF FAME:
Eunice Newton Foote
1819–1888

The climate changes caused by disruption to Earth's carbon cycle were first identified by Eunice Newton Foote, an amateur American scientist. In the 1840s, Foote explored how different gases absorb heat from sunlight and found that carbon dioxide got the hottest. She wondered what would happen to the climate if the amount of carbon dioxide in the air went up or down. Foote's work was originally ignored because she was a woman, but her findings were rediscovered in the 1970s.

Other Cycles

Living things need a supply of several chemicals to stay alive. For example, phosphorus is used in DNA and fats, and nitrogen is an essential ingredient in proteins. Plants take these nutrients from the soil, and they are passed on to animals through the food web.

Nitrogen Cycle

The air is 79 percent nitrogen, but this gas is very unreactive and hard for life to take in. The nitrogen cycle relies on bacteria to take the gas from the air and turn it into soil chemicals. Lightning also converts nitrogen gas into chemicals that dissolve in rain. Animal urine and droppings also add nitrogen to the soil. Other bacteria then reverse the process, breaking down nitrogen-rich chemicals in the soil back into pure nitrogen gas.

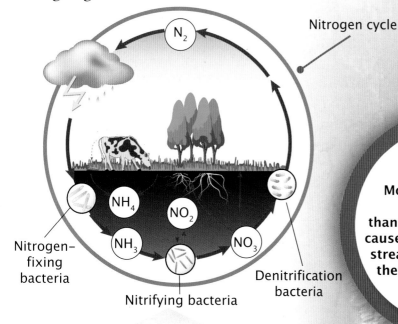

Nitrogen cycle

N_2

Nitrogen–fixing bacteria

NH_4

NH_3

NO_2

NO_3

Nitrifying bacteria

Denitrification bacteria

Most of the land on Earth is higher than the oceans. Gravity causes water to flow into streams and rivers, and then down to the sea.

HALL OF FAME:
James Lovelock
1919–2022

James Lovelock worked as a scientist and engineer for nearly 80 years. He is most remembered for his Gaia hypothesis, which is a way of understanding how the entire Earth works as a self-controlling system. Just like a living body, Lovelock described how Earth's systems maintained stable conditions—only these processes took many thousands or millions of years.

The water picks up chemicals locked in the rocks and carries them downstream. They will end up in soils where they will be used by plants and other life.

The flow of water is changing the landscape by a process called erosion. The water breaks up rocks into sand and silt, gradually carving out river valleys.

Water Cycle

All life relies on water to survive. Most of Earth's liquid water is in the oceans and soaked into rocks deep underground. However, it is always rising up from the oceans into the air, falling down again as rain, and flowing over the land back to the sea. This is called the water cycle. The water cycle is driven by the warmth of the Sun, which turns liquid water into water vapor. As this vapor cools, it turns back into liquid and falls as rain.

Although the total amount of water on Earth never changes, it is also always on the move.

DID YOU KNOW? About 96 percent of the human body is made up of just four elements: oxygen, carbon, hydrogen, and nitrogen, but there are at least 12 other elements that are essential for life.

Dry Biomes

There is a close relationship between a place's climate and the kinds of wildlife communities that survive there. The world is divided into sectors known as biomes based on this. Dry biomes, where there is not much rainfall each year, include deserts, grasslands, and also the polar ice sheets.

Camels are famous desert animals. The hump is filled with oily fats that can be used to provide the camel with food and water for several days.

Low Rain

A desert is any area where less than 25 cm (10 in) of rain falls each year. Grasslands and semi-deserts get more rain but not enough for trees and forests to grow. Low rain is sometimes caused by rain shadows, where all the moisture in the air falls as rain on one side of tall mountains. Only dry air reaches the other side. Dry lands are also found far inland where no rainclouds can reach. Large, hot deserts form in the regions either side of the Equator.

Bison live on the North American prairies, which are formed by the rain shadow of the Rocky Mountains.

Emperor penguins are the only animals to spend the winter in Antarctica. The males look after chicks at this time, while the females feed at sea.

Cold Deserts

The driest place on Earth is not the Sahara or another hot desert. Instead it is Antarctica, where it is almost always below freezing. That means all the water here is frozen and there is no liquid water at all. Very few plants and animals survive in the Antarctic desert because of the cold temperatures as well as the lack of water. Mostly, the animals here live in the ocean and only come on land to rest after feeding out at sea. They get their water from their food.

HALL OF FAME:
Vandana Shiva
1952–

Vandana Shiva is an Indian environmentalist campaigning for farmers across the world to return to traditional methods, especially in places where water and nutrients are scarce. Shiva suggests that this will boost harvests and help keep soils fertile. However, not everyone agrees with this approach and some say that chemical fertilizers and genetically modified crops will be a better way of feeding the world.

Dry biomes have few plants, and the soil lacks nutrients. Instead it is loose sand, and any rain that does fall will trickle right through.

Camels are well adapted to a life in the dry, sandy deserts of Africa and Asia. Their wide feet spread out, so they do not sink in the sand.

DID YOU KNOW? About 40 percent of the Earth's land is covered in dry biomes, like deserts and prairies, which receive less than 130 cm (51 in) of rain each year.

Wet Biomes

Land areas with high rainfall develop into either forests or wetlands. The water allows trees—large but slow-growing plants—to take over the area. If the tops of the trees form a single leafy layer, or canopy, the habitat is a forest. In woodlands, there are gaps between the trees. A wetland occurs where the rainwater cannot drain away, and so marsh or swamp forms.

Rain forest and jungles grow in tropical areas close to the equator. These areas are always warm and wet, so plants can keep growing all year round.

Boreal Forest

The world's largest forests are in cool parts of the world near the poles. Nearly all of this biome is in the northern hemisphere, and so it is called "boreal" forest (boreal means northern). For most of the year, these forests are covered in snow. The trees here are evergreen conifers, which only grow during the short summers.

The moose, the world's largest deer, lives in the boreal forest. Most big animals live in the sea or on savannas and grasslands.

HALL OF FAME:
Wangari Maathai
1940–2011

Wangari Maathai grew up in the mountains of Kenya. She set up the Green Belt Movement, which helped the people living in rural Africa—especially the women—to plant more trees and create a more fertile habitat. This tree planting restored forest areas that had been cleared for fields and created new opportunities for local people.

DID YOU KNOW? A fifth of the world's forests have been cut down in the last 100 years.

Deciduous Forest

Forests that grow in a mild climate are deciduous, which means that the trees drop their leaves before winter and grow them again in spring. This prevents the broad and thin leaves being damaged by freezing winter conditions. The spring and summer are longer and warmer here, so the trees have enough time to regrow leaves each year.

The valuable green chlorophyll is pulled out of the leaves before they are dropped for winter. The leaves change to vibrant shades of red, orange, or yellow.

The rain forests are among the oldest biomes on Earth, often many millions of years old. As a result, each small area of forest has a distinct ecosystem.

Rain forests are packed with life, and there may be 1,000 different animals species—monkeys, insects, spiders, and lizards—living in just one tree.

Ocean Zones

More than two-thirds of the surface of Earth is covered in oceans with an average depth of 3.5 km (2.15 miles). Most of the life in the ocean lives within 200 m (650 ft) of the surface and within 200 km (125 miles) of the coast.

Depth Layers

The conditions for life vary with depth. The top layer is the sunlit or epipelagic zone. This is where there is enough light during the day to photosynthesize. Next is the twilight (mesopelagic) zone, which goes down to 1,000 m (0.62 miles). Many animals stay hidden in this gloom during the day and then hunt at the surface by night. Below this is the midnight (bathypelagic) zone, where it is dark 24 hours a day.

Sardines eat plankton—floating microscopic organisms. The surface waters are filled with plankton and they are an important food source for many sea creatures.

ocean surface 0 m

Epipelagic zone
about 200 m

Mesopelagic zone
about 1,000 m

Bathypelagic zone
about 4,000 m

Abyssopelagic zone
ocean floor

Hadopelagic zone

The diversity of wildlife on the oceanic zones

No plants can live in the deep ocean. Animals that live down at the seabed are described as benthic.

This angler fish has a small glowing lure dangling over its head. Smaller fish that come to investigate will get gobbled up.

In the Deep Sea

The deep, dark oceans are a very empty place with not much to eat. Some animals rely on marine snow, which is the constant supply of fragments of waste and dead bodies that fall down from higher up. Other animals attract prey by using bioluminescence to create their own light.

The fish are all trying to wriggle into the middle of the shoal where they are safest from attack.

Sardines have mirrorlike scales that reflect back the blue of the water. This makes them hard for predators to see.

HALL OF FAME:
Sylvia Earle
1935–

An American marine biologist, Sylvia Earle is famous for her work with *National Geographic* as an explorer and educator. However, before that, Earle was a pioneer of deep–sea exploration, and helped build underwater laboratories for teams of scientists to live and work in for weeks at a time. Today, Earle is one of the Ocean Elders, a team of scientists, environmentalists, and explorers who work to protect the oceans from damage.

DID YOU KNOW? Every year, an estimated 11 million tonnes (12 million tons) of plastic is dumped in the ocean—weighing more than 200,000 blue whales.

Symbiosis

Some organisms have evolved to live in a very close relationship with another species. This is known as symbiosis. There are three types. Mutualism is where both partners benefit from the relationship. In commensalism, one organism benefits, and the other is unaffected. Finally, in parasitism, one species benefits at the cost of the other, its host.

Corals have symbiotic algae living inside them. As the seas warm, the algae leave corals, making them go white and die, a process called coral bleaching.

Lichens

The crusts that grow on rocks and bark in cold and windy parts of the world are a symbiotic partnership between a fungus and microscopic algae. The algae are inside the fungus, which provides a safe place to live. In return, the algae feeds the fungus with sugars made by photosynthesis. Other kinds of fungi buried in the soil are often in symbiosis with the plants growing at the surface.

The fungus has a hard, crusty body that stops the algae inside from drying out.

Parasite and Host

A parasite cannot live without its host, which provides it with a place to live (for at least a while) and a source of food. Hosts may not be killed by the parasite but are weakened by them. Endoparasites, like tapeworms, live inside the body, often in the digestive system or blood supply. Ectoparasites, such as fleas, live on the outside of the body.

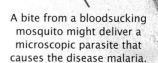

A bite from a bloodsucking mosquito might deliver a microscopic parasite that causes the disease malaria.

HALL OF FAME: Meredith Blackwell

1940–

The American researcher Meredith Blackwell is a leading expert on parasitic fungi, such as *Cordyceps*, that take over the bodies of insects. The fungus grows through the body of its host and eventually kills it. Blackwell uses an electron microscope to study this and other interesting symbiotic and parasitic fungi.

A giant clam cannot get all the food it needs by filtering seawater. It has algae living in its soft body, which contribute sugars in exchange for a place to live.

Giant clams always live in clear, shallow waters, so there is plenty of light for its symbiotic algae to photosynthesize.

DID YOU KNOW? American badgers and coyotes are symbiotic. The coyote is able to sniff out the burrow of a burrowing gopher, and the badger's job is to dig it up.

Social Groups

Some animals will spend most of their time by themselves, avoiding other member of their species. However, it is common for other animals to gather into groups. There are many reasons for crowding together, because living in groups has different benefits.

Chimpanzees live in troops made up of a mixture of relatives and friends. The apes are always arguing about who is in charge.

Herds and Flocks

Large animal groups provide safety in numbers. Seabirds gather on cliffs to breed, hoofed animals form vast herds, and fish school in tight shoals all for the same reason. Predators that attack often have difficulty singling out one individual. A solitary animal would be at greater risk. The animals are also all on the lookout for danger and will warn the others if a predator is nearby.

Seabirds like these gannets compete to nest in the middle of the colony, where it is safest.

Leaf-cutter ants do not eat leaves but feed them to a fungus garden in the nest, and then the ants eat the fungus.

Eusocial Animals

Ants, bees, and wasps are examples of eusocial animals, where a large colony of related animals work together to raise the young produced by just one member of the group. This highly organized social system is very good at keeping the colony alive during periods of drought or when food runs low. Other eusocial species include termites, which eat wood, and naked mole rats, which eat roots.

DID YOU KNOW? Locusts form very large groups called swarms. One of the largest swarms ever recorded was in 1954 and had around 10 billion insects.

Chimps communicate with calls and expressions. This face means that the chimp is unhappy about something.

The apes spend a lot of time grooming each other by cleaning away dirt from their fur. This helps to form trusting relationships.

HALL OF FAME:
Nikolaas Tinbergen
1907–1988

The Dutch zoologist Nikolaas Tinbergen was one of the first scientists to study the ways in which animals behave, a field that is now called ethology. Tinbergen wanted to understand why animals acted like they did, especially those that lived in groups. Tinbergen won the Nobel prize in 1973 for his work in revealing why social groups worked.

Glossary

AMINO ACID
An essential nutrient containing several chemical elements.

ARTERY
One of the main vessels carrying blood from the heart to other parts of the body.

ATOM
The smallest possible particle of a chemical element.

BACTERIA
A large group of single cell microorganisms, some of which cause diseases.

BIOME
A large community of life suited to a particular climate and landscape.

CARBOHYDRATE
A substance containing carbon, hydrogen and oxygen, such as a sugar or starch.

CARBON DIOXIDE (CO_2)
A waste gas produced by the body, made up of one carbon atom bonded to two oxygen atoms.

CELL
The basic unit of plants, animals, fungi, and microrganisms. Each cell has a central control, or nucleus, and is surrounded by a thin membrane.

CELLULOSE
A substance that is the chief part of the cell walls of plants and is used in making products such as paper and rayon.

CHLOROPHYLL
Chemical that green plants use to help make their food.

CLASSIFICATION
The arrangement of organisms into groups based on their similarities.

CLIMATE
The usual weather for an area over a long period of time.

DIGESTION
The process of breaking down food in the body to release essential nutrients.

DNA
Short for deoxyribonucleic acid, the chemical ingredient that forms genes. Parents pass on copied parts of their DNA to their children, so that some of their traits are also passed on.

ECOLOGY
How organisms relate to each other in their surroundings.

ECOSYSTEM
The community of interacting organisms and non-living things in a habitat.

ENDOSKELETON
An internal skeleton.

ENZYME
A chemical that speeds up or slows down the way in which substances react with each other.

EUKARYOTE
An organism that has cells with a nucleus and other separate structures surrounded by membranes.

EVAPORATE
To turn from liquid into vapor.

FAT
A chemical substance that the body produces to store energy. It is stored in fat cells beneath the skin or surrounding organs.

FOOD WEB
A series of plants and animals that depend on each other for food.

GENE
A combination of chemicals that carries information about how an organism will appear and behave.

HABITAT
The natural home environment of a plant, animal, or other living thing.

HORMONE
A chemical that helps to regulate processes such as reproduction and growth.

INHERITANCE
The passing on of characteristics to offspring from their parents.

INVERTEBRATE
An animal without a backbone.

IMMUNE SYSTEM
The network of organs, chemicals, and special cells that protects the body from disease.

MEMBRANE
A thin, flexible layer of tissue around organs or cells.

METABOLISM
The chemical processes that the body's cells use to produce energy from food, get rid of waste, and heal themselves.

MOLECULE
The smallest possible unit of a substance that still behaves like that substance. A molecule is made up of two or more atoms.

NERVE
The part of the nervous system that carries signals.

NUCLEUS
The central part of an eukaryotic cell, which controls its function and stores its DNA.

NUTRIENTS
Substances that provide food needed for life and growth.

ORGAN
A group of tissues that work together to do a specific job, such as the heart or brain.

ORGANELLE
Part of a cell that does one job.

ORGANISM
A living thing, including plants, animals, fungi, and single-celled life forms.

PHOTOSYNTHESIS
The process of plants using sunlight to create sugars out of water and carbon dioxide.

POLLINATION
The transfer of pollen so that plants can reproduce.

PREDATOR
An animal that feeds on other animals.

PROKARYOTE
A single-celled organism with no distinct nucleus or cell membrane, such as bacteria or archaea.

PROTEIN
One of the most important of all molecules in the body and in nature. Protein is needed to strengthen and replace tissue in the body.

RESPIRATION
Breathing and also the metabolic process that releases energy from sugars.

RESPIRATORY SYSTEM
The organs that are involved with breathing.

SPECIES
A group of similar-looking organisms that can reproduce together.

SPERM
A male reproductive cell that combines with a female's egg to produce a new baby.

TEMPERATURE
The degree or intensity of heat present in a substance.

TISSUE
A collection of cells that look the same and have a similar job to do in a body.

VARIATION
The differences in characteristics between individuals of the same species.

VEIN
One of the main vessels carrying blood from different parts of the body to the heart.

VERTEBRATE
An animal with a backbone.

VIRUS
A tiny organism that cannot grow or reproduce unless it is inside the cell of another organism.

VITAMIN
A natural substance found in foods that the human body cannot produce, although it is necessary for good health.

ZOOLOGY
The study of animals and animal life.

Index